Growing Success: A Comprehensive Guide to Marketing Agrochemical Products

by **Rodolfo Abelardo B. Ablazo**

Foreword

As I stand on the precipice of introducing "Growing Success: A Comprehensive Guide to Marketing Agrochemicals" to the world, I can't help but reflect on the journey that led me to this point. It's a journey marked by countless conversations with Filipino agrochemical marketers who, like me, share a deep passion for agriculture and an unwavering commitment to our nation's food security.

This book is not just the culmination of my own experiences but also the collective wisdom of those dedicated professionals who have tirelessly worked to nourish our fields, protect our crops, and sustain our communities. "Growing Success" is, at its core, a tribute to the Filipino spirit of resilience and innovation that courses through the veins of our agriculture industry.

In these pages, I've poured my heart and soul into creating a resource specifically tailored to the Filipino agrochemical marketer. It's a guide born out of a deep understanding of our unique challenges and opportunities, a roadmap for navigating the dynamic landscape of agrochemical marketing in the Philippines.

While the principles discussed in this book are universal, the application is distinctly Filipino. From the rich tapestry of our agricultural heritage to the intricacies of our local markets, "Growing Success" equips you with insights and strategies that resonate with our culture, our values, and our aspirations for our nation's agriculture.

One of the book's core missions is to shed light on the vital role that agrochemicals play in achieving food security and sustainable farming practices. It's about more than just selling products; it's about enabling farmers to thrive, ensuring that the fruits of our labor are safe and abundant, and stewarding our land for future generations.

"Growing Success" covers a wide spectrum, from the science behind agrochemicals to the art of effective marketing. It's a comprehensive resource for both seasoned industry professionals and those entering the field, offering actionable strategies and real-world examples that can transform your approach to agrochemical marketing.

As we embark on this journey together, may "Growing Success" empower you with the knowledge, tools, and inspiration to make a lasting impact on the agriculture landscape of the Philippines. Let it be your trusted companion as you navigate the challenges and seize the opportunities that lie ahead.

I extend my heartfelt gratitude to the Filipino agrochemical community, my mentors, colleagues, and every individual who has contributed to the creation of this book. Your unwavering support and dedication to our shared mission have made this endeavor possible.

In closing, I invite you to immerse yourself in "Growing Success." May it be a beacon of guidance and innovation as we work hand in hand to ensure the prosperity of Filipino agriculture, a thriving industry that sustains not only our livelihoods but also the hopes and dreams of countless families across our nation.

Rodolfo Abelardo "POLO" B. Ablazo

Mabalacat City, Pampanga

September 26, 2023

Error! Filename not specified.

Contents:

Chapter 1: Introduction to Agrochemical Marketing

- Understanding the agrochemical industry

- Market trends and challenges

- Importance of effective marketing strategies

Chapter 2: Knowing Your Target Audience

- Identifying key stakeholders

- Analyzing farmers' needs and preferences

- Segmenting the market for targeted outreach

Chapter 3: Product Development and Differentiation

- Creating innovative agrochemical products

- Highlighting unique selling points (USPs)

- Demonstrating product effectiveness through research and

trials

Chapter 4: Branding and Positioning

- Crafting a strong brand identity

- Positioning your agrochemical products in the market

- Leveraging storytelling for brand engagement

Chapter 5: Developing a Marketing Plan

- Setting clear marketing objectives

- Creating a budget and timeline

- Integrating digital and traditional marketing channels

Chapter 6: Digital Marketing Strategies

- Harnessing the power of social media

- Email marketing and automation for customer engagement

- Utilizing SEO and content marketing to reach a wider audience

Chapter 7: Building Relationships with Distributors and Retailers

- Selecting the right distribution partners

- Training and supporting retailers

- Implementing effective channel management strategies

Chapter 8: Promotional Activities and Campaigns

- Designing impactful promotional campaigns

- Organizing product demonstrations and field days

- Sponsorships, events, and trade shows for brand exposure

Chapter 9: Customer Relationship Management (CRM)

- Implementing CRM systems for better customer retention

- Personalization and customer support

- Gathering feedback and addressing concerns

Chapter 10: Sustainability and Responsible Marketing

- Embracing sustainability practices in agrochemical marketing

- Communicating environmental benefits responsibly

- Addressing safety and regulatory considerations

Chapter 11: Measuring Marketing Effectiveness

- Key performance indicators (KPIs) for agrochemical marketing

- Analyzing marketing data and making data-driven decisions

- Continuous improvement and optimization

Chapter 12: Navigating Ethical Challenges

- Ethical considerations in agrochemical marketing

- Promoting transparency and honesty

- Complying with industry regulations and standards

Conclusion

- Recap of key marketing strategies for agrochemical products

- Looking ahead to future trends and opportunities

- Empowering the agrochemical industry for sustainable growth

Chapter 1: Introduction to Agrochemical Marketing

Error! Filename not specified.

A. Understanding the Agrochemical Industry

Understanding the agrochemical industry is essential for anyone involved in marketing agrochemical products. This industry plays a pivotal role in modern agriculture by providing various chemical inputs that enhance crop yield, protect plants from pests and diseases, and promote efficient farm management. Here's an in-depth expounding on the topic:

1. **Definition and Scope:**

The agrochemical industry encompasses the production, distribution, and sale of a wide range of chemical products used in agriculture. These products include fertilizers, pesticides, herbicides, insecticides, fungicides, and other chemical agents. Additionally, it involves the development of biotechnological advancements and genetically modified organisms (GMOs) designed to improve crop traits and resistance.

2. **Importance to Agriculture:**

Agrochemicals have revolutionized agriculture, enabling farmers to meet the global food demand. They significantly contribute to improving crop productivity, protecting crops from pests and diseases, and optimizing resource utilization. Agrochemicals are instrumental in ensuring food security and supporting the livelihoods of millions of people involved in agriculture.

3. Types of Agrochemicals:

There are three main categories of agrochemicals:

A. Fertilizers: These provide essential nutrients to plants, such as nitrogen, phosphorus, and potassium, enhancing soil fertility and crop growth.

B. Pesticides: Used to control or eliminate pests, diseases, and weeds that threaten crop health and yield.

C. Plant Growth Regulators: These regulate plant growth and development, influencing various physiological processes.

4. Industry Challenges:

The agrochemical industry faces several challenges:

- **Environmental Concerns**: The potential negative impact of certain agrochemicals on the environment, such as water pollution and harm to non-target organisms.

- **Regulatory Compliance**: Strict regulations and safety standards imposed by governments and international bodies to protect human health and the environment.

- **Resistance and Sustainability**: The development of resistance in pests and diseases to certain agrochemicals, necessitating sustainable and integrated pest management practices.

- **Public Perception**: Dealing with public misconceptions and negative perceptions surrounding the use of agrochemicals.

5. **Research and Innovation:**

Constant research and innovation are crucial in the agrochemical industry to address challenges and develop safer and more effective products. This includes the discovery of novel active ingredients, advanced formulations, and biotechnological solutions.

6. Global Market and Trends:

The agrochemical industry is a global market with significant players across different regions. Market trends include the increasing adoption of biopesticides and biofertilizers, growing interest in precision agriculture technologies, and the rise of sustainable agriculture practices.

7. **Collaboration and Partnerships**:

Collaboration between agrochemical companies, research institutions, and agricultural organizations is vital for fostering innovation, ensuring responsible product use, and addressing industry challenges collectively.

8. **Consumer Safety and Education:**

Educating farmers and end consumers about proper agrochemical use, safety measures, and adherence to label instructions is essential to promote responsible application and minimize risks.

Understanding the agrochemical industry is an ongoing process as it continuously evolves with new scientific discoveries, technologies, and shifting global dynamics. As marketing professionals, comprehending these aspects empowers you to develop targeted strategies that resonate with the industry's stakeholders while promoting sustainable agricultural practices.

B. Market Trends and Challenges in Agrochemical Marketing:

Market Trends:

1. **<u>Growing Demand for Sustainable Solutions</u>**: The agriculture industry is witnessing a rising demand for agrochemical products that are environmentally friendly and promote sustainable farming practices. Consumers and regulatory bodies are increasingly concerned about the

impact of agrochemicals on ecosystems and human health. This trend has led to the development and adoption of biopesticides, biofertilizers, and other organic alternatives.

2. **Digital Transformation**: The agrochemical industry is embracing digital technologies to streamline operations, enhance communication, and improve marketing efforts. Digital platforms, including social media, websites, and mobile apps, are becoming essential tools for reaching and engaging with farmers and other stakeholders.

3. **Precision Agriculture**: Advancements in technology, such as remote sensing, GPS, and IoT devices, are revolutionizing agriculture. Precision agriculture allows farmers to apply agrochemicals with greater accuracy and efficiency, optimizing resource utilization and reducing waste. Agrochemical companies are incorporating

precision agriculture solutions into their marketing strategies to cater to tech-savvy farmers.

4. **Focus on Plant Health and Biostimulants**: Beyond traditional crop protection, agrochemical marketing is witnessing a shift towards promoting plant health and resilience. Biostimulants, which enhance plant growth and improve nutrient absorption, are gaining popularity as farmers seek ways to improve overall crop performance.

5. **Value-Added Services**: Agrochemical companies are differentiating themselves by offering value-added services such as agronomic advice, crop monitoring, and tailored solutions. Building strong relationships with farmers and providing support throughout the crop cycle enhances customer loyalty and satisfaction.

Challenges:

1. **<u>Regulatory Compliance</u>**: Agrochemical marketing is heavily regulated to ensure consumer safety and environmental protection. Companies must navigate a complex web of regulations and obtain approvals for their products, which can be time-consuming and costly.

2. **<u>Public Perception and Sustainability Concerns</u>**: Agrochemicals have faced negative public perception due to environmental and health concerns. Marketing efforts need to address these issues transparently and highlight the industry's commitment to sustainability and responsible product use.

3. **<u>Resistance and Product Efficacy</u>**: Pests and diseases can develop resistance to agrochemicals over time, reducing

product effectiveness. Marketing strategies should emphasize integrated pest management practices and innovative products designed to combat resistance.

4. **<u>Competitive Landscape</u>**: The agrochemical market is highly competitive, with numerous companies vying for market share. Differentiating products and creating a unique brand identity become critical challenges in this crowded space.

5. **<u>Education and Adoption</u>**: Farmers may be hesitant to adopt new agrochemical products and technologies due to a lack of awareness or familiarity. Effective marketing requires educational campaigns to demonstrate the benefits and proper use of products.

6. **<u>Supply Chain and Distribution</u>**: Ensuring timely and efficient distribution of agrochemical products to remote

rural areas can be challenging. Companies must collaborate with distributors and retailers to reach farmers effectively.

7. **<u>Climate Change and Uncertainty</u>**: Climate change poses risks and uncertainties for agriculture. Agrochemical marketing must adapt to changing weather patterns, extreme events, and shifting agricultural practices.

Navigating these market trends and challenges requires agrochemical companies to be adaptable, innovative, and responsive to the needs of farmers and the broader agricultural sector. By embracing sustainability, leveraging technology, and prioritizing customer education, agrochemical marketing can contribute to the advancement of modern agriculture while addressing environmental concerns and meeting regulatory requirements.

C. Importance of effective marketing strategies

Effective marketing strategies play a crucial role in the agrochemical industry, as they are essential for promoting and selling agricultural chemicals, such as fertilizers, pesticides, and herbicides. Here are some key points on the importance of these strategies:

1. **Raising Awareness**: Agrochemical marketing strategies help create awareness among farmers and other stakeholders about the benefits and proper use of agricultural chemicals. This ensures that the target

audience understands the value of these products in enhancing crop yield, preventing diseases, and improving overall agricultural practices.

2. **<u>Product Differentiation</u>**: In a competitive market, effective marketing allows agrochemical companies to differentiate their products from others. It helps highlight unique features, formulations, and benefits, enabling farmers to make informed decisions based on their specific needs.

3. **<u>Education and Training</u>**: Marketing strategies can be used to provide educational materials and training programs to farmers. Educating farmers on best practices, proper application methods, and safety measures increases the effectiveness of agrochemical usage while minimizing negative impacts on the environment and human health.

4. **<u>Building Trust and Credibility</u>**: A well-executed marketing campaign can build trust and credibility for agrochemical companies. Demonstrating commitment to product quality, research, and customer support fosters long-term relationships with farmers, distributors, and other stakeholders.

5. **<u>Market Expansion</u>**: Effective marketing strategies open doors to new markets and customer segments. By identifying emerging trends, understanding customer preferences, and tailoring messages accordingly, agrochemical companies can expand their reach and increase market share.

6. **<u>Compliance and Regulation</u>**: Agrochemical marketing strategies should also address compliance with regulatory requirements. Promotional materials must adhere to

guidelines to avoid misrepresentation or misinformation, ensuring the industry's responsible and ethical practices.

7. **<u>Innovation and Research</u>**: Successful marketing strategies encourage agrochemical companies to invest in research and innovation. By identifying market demands and customer feedback, companies can develop new and improved products that address specific challenges faced by farmers.

8. **<u>Sustainability and Environmental Awareness</u>**: Emphasizing sustainability and environmentally friendly practices in marketing campaigns fosters a positive brand image. Agrochemical companies can promote products that reduce the environmental impact and contribute to sustainable agriculture practices.

In conclusion, effective marketing strategies are vital for the agrochemical industry as they help increase product adoption, foster trust, and drive growth while promoting responsible and sustainable agricultural practices. By leveraging these strategies, agrochemical companies can make a significant impact on the global agricultural landscape.

Chapter 2: Knowing Your Target Audience

Error! Filename not specified.

A. Identifying key stakeholders

Identifying key stakeholders in the Philippine agrochemical industry is crucial for understanding the diverse network of individuals, organizations, and entities that play significant roles in shaping the industry's dynamics and outcomes. Here are some key stakeholders:

1. **<u>Government Agencies</u>**: Various government agencies in the Philippines are essential stakeholders in the agrochemical industry. These include the Department of Agriculture (DA) and the Fertilizer and Pesticide Authority (FPA), which regulate and oversee the registration, distribution, and use of agrochemical products. Their policies and guidelines influence the industry's operations and compliance.

2. **<u>Agrochemical Companies</u>**: Local and multinational agrochemical companies are major stakeholders. They are

responsible for manufacturing, marketing, and distributing fertilizers, pesticides, and other agricultural chemicals. Their innovations, product offerings, and business strategies significantly impact the industry's growth and competitiveness.

3. **Farmers and Farming Communities**: Farmers form a critical stakeholder group in the agrochemical industry. Their adoption and usage of agrochemical products influence market demand and product preferences. Understanding their needs and challenges is crucial for developing effective marketing strategies and sustainable agricultural practices.

4. **Agricultural Cooperatives and Associations**: These organizations represent the collective interests of farmers and serve as vital intermediaries between farmers and

agrochemical companies. They play a role in advocating for farmer rights, providing training and education, and facilitating access to agrochemical products.

5. **<u>Academic and Research Institutions</u>**: Universities, agricultural research centers, and educational institutions contribute to the agrochemical industry through research and development activities. Their studies on crop protection, sustainable farming practices, and product efficacy influence the industry's direction and advancements.

6. **<u>Non-Governmental Organizations (NGOs):</u>** Environmental and agricultural NGOs are stakeholders concerned with promoting sustainable and responsible agrochemical practices. They advocate for environmental protection, farmer welfare, and the safe use of agrochemicals.

7. **<u>Industry Associations</u>**: Organizations like the Crop Protection Association of the Philippines (CPAP) or the CropLife, represent the collective interests of agrochemical companies. They engage with regulators, promote industry standards, and contribute to policy advocacy.

8. **<u>Distributors and Retailers</u>**: Agrochemical distributors and retailers form a vital link between manufacturers and farmers. Their distribution networks and market insights impact the availability and accessibility of agrochemical products to end-users.

9. **<u>Consumers and Consumers' Groups</u>**: Consumers of agricultural produce are indirectly affected by the agrochemical industry. Consumer groups and advocates may voice concerns about the potential effects of

agrochemical residues on food safety and the environment.

10. **<u>Media and Public</u>**: The media and the general public are crucial stakeholders as they shape public perception, influence government policies, and can impact the industry's reputation through information dissemination and advocacy.

Understanding the roles, interests, and concerns of these key stakeholders is essential for developing effective policies, sustainable practices, and successful business strategies within the Philippine agrochemical industry. Collaboration among stakeholders is vital to ensure the industry's growth while addressing environmental, social, and economic challenges.

B. Analyzing farmers' needs and preferences

Analyzing Filipino farmers' needs and preferences is essential for developing targeted and effective agricultural solutions that can address their specific challenges and improve their livelihoods. Several factors contribute to understanding their needs and preferences:

1. **Crop Diversity and Farming Practices**: Filipino farmers cultivate a wide range of crops across different regions and agro-climatic zones. Analyzing their crop preferences and traditional farming practices can help in developing crop-specific solutions and improved farming techniques tailored to their needs.

2. **Land Size and Ownership**: Farm sizes in the Philippines vary significantly, from smallholder farms to larger estates.

The needs and preferences of farmers can differ based on their land size, ownership, and access to resources.

3. **<u>Access to Technology and Information</u>**: Understanding farmers' access to agricultural technologies, such as modern machinery, irrigation systems, and information sources, is crucial. It helps identify areas where technology adoption can be enhanced to improve productivity and efficiency.

4. **<u>Financial Constraints</u>**: Many Filipino farmers face financial constraints, limiting their ability to invest in modern inputs like agrochemicals and hybrid seeds. Analyzing their financial situation can aid in designing affordable and accessible agricultural solutions.

5. **<u>Climate and Weather Patterns</u>**: The Philippines is prone to various weather-related challenges, such as typhoons, droughts, and flooding. Analyzing how these patterns affect farmers and their preferences for climate-resilient crops and practices is vital.

6. **<u>Market Demand and Price Fluctuations</u>**: Farmers' decisions on crop choices can be influenced by market demand and price fluctuations. Understanding their preferences in response to market dynamics helps in creating a more stable and sustainable agricultural sector.

7. **<u>Education and Training</u>**: Farmers' level of education and training in agricultural practices can impact their needs and preferences. Offering educational programs and extension services can enhance their knowledge and improve decision-making.

8. **<u>Pest and Disease Management</u>**: Identifying prevalent pests and diseases in different regions and farmers' current pest management practices can lead to the development of effective and targeted solutions.

9. **<u>Sustainable Agriculture</u>**: Many farmers in the Philippines are increasingly concerned about sustainability and environmental impacts. Analyzing their preferences for eco-friendly practices and products can promote the adoption of sustainable agriculture.

10. **<u>Government Policies and Support</u>**: Government interventions, subsidies, and support programs can influence farmers' needs and preferences. Understanding their perceptions of government policies can help in refining and improving these programs.

Conducting surveys, focus groups, and field studies are common methods used to gather data on farmers' needs and preferences. Engaging with agricultural cooperatives, NGOs, and extension services can also provide valuable insights. By understanding and analyzing the specific needs and preferences of Filipino farmers, policymakers, researchers, and agribusinesses can work collaboratively to develop and implement tailored solutions that contribute to the sustainable development of agriculture in the Philippines.

C. Segmenting the market for targeted outreach

Segmenting the Philippine agrochemical market is a strategic approach that involves dividing the market into distinct groups based on common characteristics, needs, and preferences. This segmentation allows agrochemical companies to design targeted outreach efforts, marketing strategies, and product offerings that better resonate with specific customer segments. Here's how segmentation can be done:

1. **<u>Geographic Segmentation</u>**: Dividing the market based on geographic regions, such as Luzon, Visayas, and Mindanao, or specific provinces and municipalities. Each region may have unique agricultural practices, crops grown, and climate conditions, leading to varying agrochemical needs.

2. **<u>Crop-Specific Segmentation</u>**: Segmenting the market based on the types of crops grown by farmers. Different crops may require specific agrochemical inputs, making it essential to tailor product promotions and information to the needs of farmers growing particular crops.

3. **<u>Farm Size Segmentation</u>**: Differentiating between smallholder farmers and large-scale agricultural enterprises. The needs, preferences, and purchasing capacity of these segments can vary significantly, influencing their agrochemical usage.

4. **<u>Technology Adoption Segmentation</u>**: Segmenting based on the level of technology adoption by farmers. Some farmers may be early adopters of modern agricultural practices and technologies, while others might prefer traditional methods. Tailoring outreach efforts to these preferences can foster better adoption rates.

5. **<u>Environmental Sustainability Segmentation</u>**: Identifying farmers who prioritize environmentally friendly and sustainable agricultural practices. Targeted outreach can

focus on promoting eco-friendly agrochemicals and sustainable farming techniques.

6. **Demographic Segmentation**: Considering demographic factors such as age, gender, and education levels can offer insights into the preferences and decision-making processes of farmers.

7. **Market Experience Segmentation**: Segmenting based on the farmers' experience and familiarity with agrochemical products. Novice farmers might need more educational outreach, while experienced farmers may seek advanced solutions.

8. **Market Behavior Segmentation**: Analyzing farmers' buying behavior and purchase patterns to identify potential

segments with specific preferences or loyalty to certain brands.

9. **Value Chain Segmentation**: Considering the various stakeholders involved in the agrochemical distribution chain, including wholesalers, retailers, and cooperatives. Different outreach strategies may be needed for each segment.

10. **Market Influencers Segmentation**: Identifying influencers and key decision-makers within the agricultural community, such as agricultural extension workers, agronomists, and farmer associations. Targeted outreach to these influencers can lead to broader market impact.

Segmenting the Philippine agrochemical market requires collecting and analyzing relevant data, such as surveys, market research, and customer feedback. Once the segments are identified, agrochemical companies can create tailored marketing messages, product bundles, and distribution channels to reach each segment effectively. This targeted outreach approach can lead to increased customer engagement, improved product adoption, and a more sustainable and profitable agrochemical market in the Philippines.

Error! Filename not specified.

Creating innovative agrochemical products

Creating innovative agrochemical products is a crucial aspect of the agricultural industry's progress. Innovative products aim to address the evolving challenges faced by farmers, promote sustainable agriculture practices, and enhance overall crop productivity. Here are some key factors and approaches involved in creating innovative agrochemical products:

1. **Research and Development (R&D):** Investing in robust research and development is essential for generating new ideas and technologies. R&D helps identify novel active ingredients, formulations, and delivery systems that can

improve the efficiency and safety of agrochemical products.

2. **<u>Targeted Solutions</u>**: Understanding the specific needs of farmers and their crops is critical in designing agrochemical products that target specific pests, diseases, and nutritional deficiencies. Targeted solutions can minimize off-target effects, reducing environmental impact and optimizing resource usage.

3. **<u>Sustainability and Environment-Friendly Formulations</u>**: Innovation in agrochemicals involves creating products with reduced environmental impact. This includes developing biopesticides, biostimulants, and organic fertilizers that promote sustainable farming practices and safeguard biodiversity.

4. **<u>Crop Protection</u>**: Developing agrochemicals that protect crops from a broad range of pests and diseases is crucial. Innovative products can have multiple modes of action, reducing the likelihood of pest resistance and enhancing long-term effectiveness.

5. **<u>Precision Agriculture</u>**: Integrating agrochemicals with precision agriculture technologies can optimize their application, ensuring that the right amount is used in the right place and at the right time. This can lead to cost savings, reduced waste, and improved efficacy.

6. **<u>Biotechnology and Genetic Modification</u>**: Biotechnological advancements, such as genetically modified crops with built-in pest resistance, can complement agrochemical products by providing more durable and sustainable solutions.

7. **<u>Adjuvants and Delivery Systems</u>**: Innovations in adjuvants and delivery systems can improve the effectiveness of agrochemicals by enhancing their absorption and distribution within plant tissues.

8. **<u>Smart Formulations</u>**: Smart formulations can release agrochemicals gradually, providing prolonged protection and nutrient supply, reducing the need for frequent applications.

9. **<u>Resistance Management</u>**: Developing products and strategies that mitigate pest and disease resistance is critical for ensuring the long-term effectiveness of agrochemicals.

10. **Collaboration and Partnerships**: Collaborating with agricultural experts, research institutions, and farmers can provide valuable insights and feedback during product development, leading to solutions that are more aligned with real-world needs.

11. **Regulatory Compliance**: Adhering to regulatory requirements and safety standards is essential in the development of innovative agrochemical products. This ensures that the products are safe for humans, non-target organisms, and the environment.

In conclusion, creating innovative agrochemical products requires a multidisciplinary approach, combining cutting-edge research, technology integration, and a deep understanding of farmers' needs and sustainability goals. By focusing on targeted solutions, sustainability, and precision agriculture, the agricultural industry can continuously improve and advance with the development of innovative agrochemical products.

Highlighting unique selling points (USPs)

Highlighting unique selling points (USPs) for agrochemical products is essential to differentiate them from competitors and attract the attention of potential customers, including farmers, distributors, and agricultural cooperatives. USPs showcase the distinct features, benefits, and advantages of the products, compelling customers to choose them over alternatives. Here are some key points to highlight as unique selling points for agrochemical products:

1. **Effective Pest and Disease Control**: Emphasize the product's efficacy in controlling a wide range of pests and diseases that

commonly affect crops. Highlighting its ability to reduce crop losses and enhance yield can be a compelling USP.

2. **Targeted Solutions**: If the agrochemical product is designed for specific crops or pests, emphasize how it addresses the unique challenges faced by farmers growing those crops.

3. **Residual Activity**: If the product offers long-lasting protection or residual activity, showcase how it can provide sustained pest control over an extended period, reducing the need for frequent applications.

4. **Environmental Safety**: If the product has a reduced environmental impact or is eco-friendly, highlight its safety for non-target organisms, water sources, and beneficial insects.

5. **<u>Nutrient Formulations</u>**: For fertilizers and nutrient products, focus on specialized formulations that ensure optimal nutrient uptake and plant growth.

6. **<u>Crop-Specific Nutrients</u>**: If the product contains essential nutrients tailored to specific crops, emphasize how it can meet the precise nutritional needs of those crops.

7. **<u>Water Efficiency</u>**: If the agrochemical product enhances water use efficiency, highlight how it can help farmers conserve water resources and improve drought resistance in crops.

8. **<u>Resistance Management:</u>** If the product employs a unique mode of action to combat resistance, showcase how it can contribute to sustainable pest management practices.

9. **<u>User-Friendly Application</u>**: If the product offers ease of application or compatibility with various application methods, emphasize how it simplifies farmers' tasks and saves time and labor.

10. **<u>Weather Resistance</u>**: For products designed to withstand adverse weather conditions, emphasize their reliability and consistency in providing crop protection.

11. **<u>Certifications and Safety Standards</u>**: Highlight any certifications, safety testing, or compliance with agricultural regulations to instill confidence in the product's quality and safety.

12. **<u>Compatibility with Integrated Pest Management (IPM)</u>**: If the product complements IPM practices, showcase how it fits into a holistic and sustainable crop protection approach.

13. **<u>Yield Enhancement</u>**: If the agrochemical product has been proven to increase crop yield or quality, present data and case studies that demonstrate its positive impact.

14. **<u>Research and Development</u>**: If the product is backed by extensive research and development efforts, showcase the expertise and investment put into its development.

15. **<u>Customer Testimonials</u>**: Include testimonials from satisfied customers or case studies that demonstrate the product's effectiveness in real-world farming scenarios.

By highlighting these unique selling points in marketing materials, product labels, and promotional campaigns, agrochemical companies can effectively communicate the value of their products to the target audience and gain a competitive edge in the market.

Demonstrating product effectiveness through research and trials

Demonstrating agrochemical product effectiveness through research and trials is crucial for building credibility, gaining regulatory approvals, and convincing farmers and stakeholders of the product's value. Rigorous scientific research and well-designed trials provide objective evidence of a product's performance, safety, and benefits. Here's why research and trials are essential and how they can be conducted effectively:

Importance of Research and Trials:

1. **Credibility and Trust**: Research and trials conducted by reputable institutions or organizations add credibility to the

product's claims. Independent studies carry more weight and instill trust in the product's effectiveness.

2. **<u>Regulatory Compliance:</u>** Regulatory authorities often require scientific data to approve the registration and commercialization of agrochemical products. Research and trials are essential for meeting regulatory requirements.

3. **<u>Evidence-Based Decision Making</u>**: Data from research and trials enable evidence-based decision making for farmers, agronomists, and agricultural advisors. They can make informed choices about product selection based on objective results.

4. **<u>Market Differentiation</u>**: Demonstrating superior performance through research and trials can set the product

apart from competitors. Unique advantages can be highlighted to attract customers.

5. **Product Improvement**: Research findings can lead to product refinements and enhancements based on identified strengths and weaknesses. Continuous improvement can optimize the product's effectiveness.

Effective Conduct of Research and Trials:

1. **Controlled Experiments**: Design trials with control groups to compare the agrochemical product's performance against existing standards or untreated plots. This allows for accurate comparisons and statistical analysis.

2. **Randomized Design**: Randomly assign treatments to different plots or fields to reduce bias and ensure the validity of results.

3. **Replication and Sample Size**: Replicate trials across multiple locations, seasons, and soil types to account for variability and enhance the generalizability of the findings. Larger sample sizes improve statistical significance.

4. **Data Collection**: Implement robust data collection protocols to ensure accurate and consistent recording of observations and measurements.

5. **Monitoring Parameters**: Measure relevant parameters such as crop yield, pest/disease control, plant health, environmental impact, and economic returns to comprehensively assess product effectiveness.

6. **Adherence to Good Agricultural Practices**: Follow recommended application rates and application methods to

ensure the product is used as intended, reflecting real-world conditions.

7. **Long-Term Studies**: Conduct long-term studies to evaluate the product's performance over multiple growing seasons and assess any potential accumulative effects.

8. **Publication and Peer Review**: Publish the research findings in peer-reviewed journals or make them publicly available. Peer review adds further validation to the study's methodology and results.

9. **Transparency**: Be transparent about the research methodology, data collection, and analysis. Share research protocols and data with relevant stakeholders.

10. **<u>Collaboration</u>**: Collaborate with academic institutions, agricultural research centers, and extension services to conduct trials with scientific rigor and independence.

By demonstrating agrochemical product effectiveness through well-executed research and trials, agrochemical companies can substantiate their product claims, earn the trust of customers, and contribute to sustainable and informed agricultural practices.

Chapter 4: Branding and Positioning

Crafting a strong brand identity

Crafting a strong brand identity for agrochemical products is essential to establish a distinct and memorable presence in the market, build customer loyalty, and differentiate products from competitors. A well-defined brand identity creates a positive perception, communicates key messages, and influences the overall success of the product. Here are some key elements and strategies to consider when crafting a strong brand identity for agrochemical products:

1. **Brand Positioning**: Define the unique positioning of the agrochemical product in the market. Identify the target audience, understand their needs, and align the product's benefits with their preferences. Position the product as a

solution to specific challenges faced by farmers, such as crop protection, yield enhancement, or sustainable farming practices.

2. **Brand Name and Logo**: Choose a distinctive and meaningful brand name that reflects the product's purpose or benefits. Design a professional and visually appealing logo that represents the product's identity and can be easily recognized.

3. **Brand Messaging**: Develop clear and compelling brand messages that convey the product's value proposition. Focus on the product's strengths, key features, and unique selling points. Consistency in messaging across marketing materials is crucial for brand recognition.

4. **Visual Identity**: Establish a consistent visual identity through color schemes, typography, and imagery. The visual elements

should evoke the desired emotions and perceptions associated with the product.

5. **Packaging Design**: Pay attention to product packaging, as it serves as the product's first point of contact with customers. Design packaging that is informative, visually appealing, and aligns with the brand identity.

6. **Brand Storytelling**: Create a brand story that communicates the product's origins, mission, and commitment to quality. Humanize the brand by sharing stories of farmers benefiting from the product's use.

7. **Consistency in Communication**: Ensure consistency in all communication channels, including advertising, social media, website, and promotional materials. This consistency reinforces the brand's identity and message.

8. **Engage with Customers**: Establish a strong online and offline presence to engage with customers. Respond to inquiries promptly, provide helpful content, and foster a community around the brand.

9. **Customer Testimonials and Case Studies**: Showcase success stories from satisfied customers through testimonials and case studies. Real-life experiences add credibility to the brand and its effectiveness.

10. **Environmental Responsibility**: If the agrochemical product promotes sustainability and environmental responsibility, emphasize this in the brand identity. Highlight eco-friendly practices and certifications.

11. **<u>Educational Content</u>**: Offer educational content, such as blogs, videos, and webinars, that provide valuable information to farmers. Position the brand as an authority in agricultural knowledge.

12. **<u>Customer Support and Training</u>**: Provide excellent customer support and training materials to help farmers make the most of the product. Demonstrating ongoing commitment to customer success reinforces the brand's identity.

13. **<u>Innovative Initiatives</u>**: If the product incorporates innovative technologies or methodologies, showcase these initiatives to position the brand as forward-thinking and cutting-edge.

By carefully crafting a strong brand identity, agrochemical products can create a lasting and positive impression on their target audience. A consistent and well-defined brand identity will help in gaining customer trust, establishing brand loyalty, and achieving long-term success in the agrochemical market.

Positioning your agrochemical products in the market

Positioning agrochemical products in the Philippine market is crucial for establishing a strong presence, attracting the target audience, and gaining a competitive advantage. Effective positioning helps differentiate the products from competitors and communicates their unique value proposition. Here are some key strategies to consider when positioning agrochemical products in the Philippine market:

1. **<u>Market Segmentation</u>**: Identify specific target segments within the Philippine agricultural industry based on factors like crop types, farm sizes, geographic regions, and farming

practices. Tailor the product positioning to address the unique needs and preferences of each segment.

2. **Value Proposition**: Clearly define the product's value proposition – the unique benefits and advantages it offers to Filipino farmers. Highlight how the agrochemical product addresses specific challenges, improves crop yield, and contributes to sustainable agriculture practices.

3. **Quality and Safety Assurance**: Emphasize the product's quality, safety, and compliance with local regulations. Filipino farmers prioritize the safety of their crops and the environment, making it essential to position the product as reliable and compliant with industry standards.

4. **Environmental Sustainability**: If the agrochemical product promotes sustainable and eco-friendly practices, highlight its

positive impact on the environment and soil health. Position the product as a responsible choice for farmers who prioritize sustainability.

5. Crop-**Specific Solutions**: Position the agrochemical product as a specialized solution for specific crops or pests commonly found in the Philippines. Demonstrating its efficacy in targeting crop-specific challenges can attract farmers seeking tailored solutions.

6. **Innovation and Technology**: If the product incorporates innovative technologies or formulations, showcase its cutting-edge features. Position the brand as a leader in agricultural innovation, appealing to forward-thinking farmers.

7. **Collaboration and Support**: Highlight the brand's commitment to supporting Filipino farmers through

educational initiatives, extension services, and training programs. Position the product as part of a holistic support system for farmers.

8. **<u>Competitive Pricing</u>**: Offer competitive pricing strategies, especially for cost-sensitive markets like the Philippines. Position the product as a high-value solution that justifies its cost in terms of improved crop yield and performance.

9. **<u>Customer Testimonials and Success Stories</u>**: Share testimonials and case studies from satisfied Filipino farmers who have experienced positive results using the product. These real-life experiences add credibility to the positioning.

10. **<u>Distribution Network</u>**: Strengthen the distribution network to ensure easy accessibility of the product to farmers across

different regions of the Philippines. Position the brand as a reliable and accessible partner for farmers.

11. **<u>Local Partnerships</u>**: Collaborate with local agricultural organizations, cooperatives, and extension services to reinforce the brand's commitment to the Philippine agricultural community.

12. **<u>Marketing Channels</u>**: Utilize a mix of traditional and digital marketing channels to reach the target audience effectively. Engage in social media campaigns, attend agricultural events, and participate in farmer workshops.

13. **<u>Continuous Research and Development</u>**: Demonstrate the brand's ongoing commitment to research and development to improve product effectiveness continually. Position the product as part of a dynamic and evolving solution for farmers.

By carefully positioning agrochemical products in the Philippine market, agrochemical companies can align their offerings with the needs and aspirations of Filipino farmers. Effective positioning can lead to increased product adoption, customer loyalty, and a strong brand reputation in the Philippine agricultural industry.

Leveraging storytelling for brand engagement

Leveraging storytelling for agrochemical brand engagement can be a powerful and effective strategy to connect with the target audience, including farmers, distributors, and agricultural stakeholders. Storytelling creates an emotional connection with the audience, making the brand more relatable and memorable. Here are some ways to use storytelling to engage the audience and strengthen the agrochemical brand:

1. **Humanize the Brand**: Share stories that humanize the agrochemical brand by featuring the experiences of farmers, agronomists, or agricultural experts who have benefited from using the products. Highlighting personal anecdotes and challenges faced on the farm can create empathy and build rapport with the audience.

2. **Showcase Success Stories**: Share success stories of farmers who have achieved significant improvements in crop yield and quality after using the agrochemical products. Use real data and testimonials to substantiate the success, making the brand's impact tangible and credible.

3. **<u>Highlight Environmental Impact</u>**: Share stories that emphasize the agrochemical brand's commitment to environmental sustainability. Showcase how the products promote responsible and eco-friendly farming practices, preserving the environment for future generations.

4. **<u>Educational Narratives</u>**: Use storytelling as a means to educate farmers about best practices, application techniques, and the benefits of using agrochemical products. Engaging narratives can make educational content more engaging and easier to understand.

5. **<u>Historical Narratives</u>**: Uncover the brand's history and heritage through storytelling. Share anecdotes of the brand's journey, milestones, and contributions to agriculture over the years, showcasing its expertise and commitment to the industry.

6. **<u>Behind-the-Scenes Stories</u>**: Take the audience behind the scenes of the agrochemical brand's research and development efforts. Share stories of scientists, agronomists, and experts working passionately to develop innovative and effective solutions.

7. **<u>Local Community Impact</u>**: Highlight the positive impact of the agrochemical brand on local farming communities. Share stories of how the brand's initiatives have improved the livelihoods of farmers, contributed to rural development, or empowered women in agriculture.

8. **<u>Animated Videos</u>**: Use animated videos to present captivating stories related to the brand's products and their benefits. Animation can be a powerful medium to simplify complex concepts and engage the audience visually.

9. **<u>Social Media Campaigns</u>**: Run social media campaigns that revolve around storytelling. Encourage farmers to share their experiences with the brand through user-generated content, fostering a sense of community and advocacy.

10. **<u>Incorporate Visuals:</u>** Complement storytelling with visual elements like images and infographics to enhance the narrative's impact and make it more shareable across different platforms.

11. **<u>Transparency and Ethical Narratives</u>**: Share stories that showcase the brand's transparency, ethical practices, and commitment to customer safety and satisfaction. Transparency builds trust and fosters a positive brand reputation.

12. **<u>Consistent Brand Voice</u>**: Maintain a consistent brand voice throughout the storytelling process. This helps reinforce the brand identity and ensures that all stories align with the brand's core values and messaging.

By leveraging storytelling in their brand engagement efforts, agrochemical companies can create a meaningful connection with their audience, fostering brand loyalty, and advocating for sustainable and responsible agricultural practices. Well-crafted stories have the potential to leave a lasting impression on the audience and position the agrochemical brand as a trusted and valued partner in the farming community.

Chapter 5: Developing a Marketing Plan

Error! Filename not specified.

Setting clear marketing objectives

Setting clear marketing objectives for agrochemical products is essential for guiding the marketing efforts, measuring success, and aligning the team's efforts with the overall business goals. Well-defined marketing objectives provide a roadmap for the marketing strategy, ensuring that resources are utilized effectively. Here's why clear marketing objectives are crucial and how they can be established for agrochemical products:

Importance of Clear Marketing Objectives:

1. **Focus and Direction**: Clear marketing objectives help the marketing team focus on specific outcomes and activities that contribute to the product's success in the market.

2. **Measurable Outcomes**: Objectives that are specific and measurable allow for tracking progress and evaluating the success of marketing campaigns.

3. **Alignment with Business Goals**: Setting marketing objectives that align with the overall business goals ensures that marketing efforts contribute to the company's growth and profitability.

4. **Resource Allocation**: Well-defined objectives help in allocating resources effectively, ensuring that budget, time, and efforts are channeled towards achieving the desired outcomes.

5. **Performance Evaluation**: Clear marketing objectives provide a basis for evaluating the marketing team's performance and identifying areas for improvement.

6. **Adaptability**: Objectives that are clear and measurable facilitate adaptability in the marketing strategy, allowing the team to make data-driven decisions and adjustments when needed.

Establishing Clear Marketing Objectives for Agrochemical Products:

1. **Increase Product Awareness**: Set objectives to raise awareness about the agrochemical product among the target audience. This could include increasing brand visibility, website traffic, and social media engagement.

2. **<u>Improve Market Share</u>**: Establish objectives to gain a specific percentage of market share within a defined timeframe. This could involve increasing sales or capturing a larger share of the target segment.

3. **<u>Promote Product Differentiation</u>**: Set objectives to communicate the unique selling points (USPs) of the agrochemical product to position it as distinct from competitors.

4. **<u>Expand Distribution Reach</u>**: Objectives can focus on increasing the product's availability by expanding the distribution network to reach more farmers and agricultural retailers.

5. **Enhance Customer Engagement**: Establish objectives to improve customer engagement through educational content, social media interactions, and personalized communications.

6. **Boost Sales Revenue**: Set specific revenue targets for the agrochemical product over a certain period, taking into account seasonality and market trends.

7. **Encourage Product Adoption**: Objectives can be directed towards increasing the adoption rate of the product among farmers by promoting its benefits and providing support and training.

8. **Promote Sustainable Agriculture**: Set objectives to highlight the product's role in promoting sustainable agricultural practices and aligning with environmentally responsible farming methods.

9. **<u>Educate Target Audience</u>**: Establish objectives to educate the target audience about the proper and safe use of the agrochemical product through workshops, webinars, or educational materials.

10. **<u>Gain Testimonials and Case Studies</u>**: Set objectives to gather positive testimonials and case studies from satisfied customers to use in marketing materials and build trust with potential buyers.

When setting marketing objectives for agrochemical products, it's essential to ensure that they are SMART: Specific, Measurable, Achievable, Relevant, and Time-bound. This approach allows for clearer communication, effective planning, and meaningful results that contribute to the overall success of the product in the agricultural market.

Creating a budget and timeline

Creating a budget and timeline for your agrochemical marketing plan is a crucial step in ensuring the successful execution of your marketing efforts. Here's an in-depth guide to help you get started:

1. **Market Research and Analysis**:

- Begin by conducting thorough market research to understand your target audience, competitors, and industry trends.

- Allocate resources for market research, including surveys, focus groups, and data analysis.

2. **Setting Marketing Objectives**:

- Clearly define your marketing objectives, such as increasing market share, launching new products, or expanding into new regions.

- Ensure your objectives are specific, measurable, achievable, relevant, and time-bound (SMART).

3. **Budget Allocation**:

- Determine the total budget for your agrochemical marketing plan based on the objectives and market research insights.

- Allocate the budget across different marketing channels, including digital marketing, advertising, trade shows, promotions, and public relations.

4. **Digital Marketing**:

- Set aside a portion of the budget for digital marketing strategies, such as creating and optimizing a website, search engine optimization (SEO), and social media marketing.

5. **<u>Advertising and Promotions</u>**:

- Allocate funds for advertising campaigns, including online ads, print media, and outdoor advertising.

- Consider promotions, discounts, and incentives to attract new customers and retain existing ones.

6. **<u>Trade Shows and Events</u>**:

- Plan for participation in relevant trade shows, conferences, and events to showcase your agrochemical products and build industry connections.

- Include expenses for booth rentals, travel, and promotional materials.

7. **<u>Public Relations and Branding</u>**:

- Budget for public relations efforts, including press releases, media relations, and influencer marketing.

- Set aside funds for branding activities to establish a strong and consistent brand identity.

8. **<u>Timeline and Milestones</u>**:

- Develop a detailed timeline outlining the start and end dates of each marketing activity.

- Set milestones and checkpoints to monitor the progress and make necessary adjustments to the plan.

9. **<u>Measurement and Analysis</u>**:

- Allocate a portion of the budget for tools and resources to measure the effectiveness of your marketing strategies.

- Analyze key performance indicators (KPIs) regularly to evaluate the success of the marketing plan.

10. **<u>Contingency Plan</u>**:

- Be prepared for unforeseen circumstances by setting aside a contingency budget to address any unexpected challenges.

Remember, creating a budget and timeline for your agrochemical marketing plan requires a careful balance between financial resources and marketing objectives. Regularly review and adapt your plan based on market feedback and performance metrics to maximize its impact and achieve your desired outcomes.

Integrating digital and traditional marketing channels

Integrating digital and traditional marketing channels in your agrochemical marketing plan is a powerful strategy to reach a wider audience, enhance brand visibility, and drive business growth. Here's an in-depth exploration of how these channels can complement each other:

1. **<u>Understanding Digital Marketing Channels</u>**:

- Digital marketing includes various channels such as websites, search engine optimization (SEO), social media, email marketing, content marketing, and online advertising.

- These channels offer the advantage of precise targeting, real-time data, and the ability to engage with the audience interactively.

2. **<u>Leveraging Traditional Marketing Channels</u>**:

- Traditional marketing channels encompass methods like print advertising, radio and TV commercials, direct mail, outdoor billboards, and event sponsorships.

- Traditional marketing often provides broad exposure and can be particularly effective in reaching specific local or rural markets.

3. **Creating a Consistent Brand Message**:

- Integrating digital and traditional marketing requires a cohesive brand message across all channels.

- Ensure that your brand's values, mission, and unique selling propositions are communicated consistently to build a strong brand identity.

4. **Utilizing Digital Platforms for Awareness**:

- Leverage digital channels like social media and content marketing to create awareness about your agrochemical products among a broader audience.

- hare valuable content, educational resources, and success stories to establish your brand as an industry expert.

5. Driving Engagement and Interaction:

- Engage with your target audience through social media platforms, responding to inquiries and feedback promptly.

- Utilize interactive content like polls, quizzes, and contests to encourage participation and strengthen customer relationships.

6. Implementing Targeted Advertising:

- Use digital advertising tools like Google Ads and social media ads to target specific demographics, interests, and geographic locations.

- Targeted advertising helps optimize ad spending by reaching those most likely to be interested in your agrochemical products.

7. <u>**Integrating QR Codes and Short URLs**</u>:

- Bridge the gap between digital and traditional marketing by incorporating QR codes or short URLs in print materials.

- These codes can direct prospects to specific webpages, product pages, or landing pages for more information or promotional offers.

8. <u>**Monitoring and Analyzing Performance**</u>:

- Utilize analytics tools to track the performance of both digital and traditional marketing efforts.

- Analyzing data helps identify which channels are driving the most engagement and conversions, enabling you to make data-driven decisions.

9. **Retargeting and Remarketing:**

- Implement retargeting strategies to re-engage potential customers who have shown interest but not yet converted.

- Use targeted ads on digital platforms to remind them of your agrochemical products and encourage them to take action.

By integrating digital and traditional marketing channels, your agrochemical marketing plan can achieve a comprehensive and effective approach. Remember that the combination of these strategies allows you to tap into various customer segments, maximize brand exposure, and ultimately boost sales and brand loyalty.

Chapter 6: Digital Marketing Strategies

Error! Filename not specified.

Harnessing the power of social media

Harnessing the power of social media in your agrochemical marketing plan can be a game-changer, enabling you to connect with your target audience, build brand awareness, and foster customer loyalty. Here's an in-depth exploration of how social media can be utilized effectively:

1. **<u>Identifying Relevant Platforms:</u>**

- Research and identify the social media platforms where your target audience is most active. Common platforms for the agriculture industry include Facebook, Twitter, LinkedIn, Instagram, and YouTube.

- Tailor your content and approach based on the preferences of each platform's user base.

2. **<u>Creating Compelling Content</u>:**

- Develop high-quality and engaging content that provides value to your audience. Share informative posts, product updates, success stories, and industry news.

- Use visuals such as images and videos to grab attention and communicate effectively.

3. **<u>Engaging with Your Audience:</u>**

- Actively respond to comments, messages, and mentions from your audience. Engaging with users shows that you care about their opinions and fosters a positive relationship.

- Encourage discussions, ask questions, and conduct polls to encourage interaction and feedback.

4. **<u>Utilizing Influencer Marketing</u>**:

- Collaborate with influencers and experts in the agricultural field to promote your agrochemical products.

- Influencers can help amplify your brand message and reach new audiences who trust their recommendations.

5. **<u>Running Targeted Advertising Campaigns</u>**:

- Utilize social media advertising to target specific demographics, interests, and geographic locations.

- Social media platforms offer detailed targeting options to ensure your ads reach the most relevant audience.

6. **<u>Showcasing Customer Testimonials</u>**:

- Share customer testimonials and success stories to showcase the effectiveness of your agrochemical products.

- Positive reviews and testimonials from satisfied customers build trust and credibility for your brand.

7. **<u>Educational and Informative Content</u>**:

- Use social media to educate your audience about the benefits and proper usage of your agrochemical products.

- Provide tips, tutorials, and guides that demonstrate your expertise in the field.

8. **<u>Running Contests and Giveaways</u>**:

- Organize contests and giveaways to generate excitement and encourage user participation.

- Contests can help increase brand visibility and engagement, leading to a larger social media following.

9. **<u>Monitoring and Analyzing Performance</u>**:

- Use social media analytics tools to track the performance of your posts, ads, and overall social media presence.

- Analyze data to identify successful strategies and areas for improvement.

10. **<u>Consistency and Timing</u>**:

- Maintain a consistent posting schedule to keep your audience engaged.

- Post at optimal times when your target audience is most active to maximize reach and interaction.

By harnessing the power of social media, your agrochemical marketing plan can build a strong online presence, establish your brand as an industry authority, and foster meaningful connections with your customers. Remember to adapt your approach based on the preferences and behaviors of your target audience to make the most of social media's potential.

Email marketing and automation for customer engagement

Email marketing and automation can be invaluable tools for customer engagement in your agrochemical marketing plan. By leveraging these strategies effectively, you can nurture relationships with your audience, provide personalized experiences, and drive sales. Here's a comprehensive exploration of their benefits and implementation:

1. **Building and Segmenting Email Lists**:

- Create an email list by capturing leads through website sign-ups, social media, and offline events.

- Segment your email list based on customer preferences, purchase history, location, or any other relevant criteria to deliver targeted content.

2. **Personalization and Customization:**

- Use customer data to personalize emails with recipients' names, location-specific offers, and product recommendations.

- Customized content makes customers feel valued and increases the likelihood of engagement.

3. **Welcome Emails and Onboarding Sequences**:

- Send welcome emails to new subscribers and customers, introducing your brand and highlighting key products or services.

- Onboarding sequences can guide customers through their first interactions with your agrochemical products, helping them achieve success.

4. **Promotional Campaigns and Offers**:

- Send out promotional emails for product launches, seasonal offers, discounts, and special events.

- Limited-time offers and exclusive deals can create a sense of urgency and drive conversions.

5. **Educational Content and Newsletters**:

- Share educational content like blog posts, guides, and industry news through newsletters.

- Position your brand as an authority in the agrochemical industry and provide valuable insights to your audience.

6. **<u>Abandoned Cart Recovery</u>**:

- Implement automated email sequences to remind customers about items left in their shopping carts.

- Abandoned cart emails can significantly increase conversion rates and recover potentially lost sales.

7. **<u>Post-Purchase Follow-ups</u>**:

- Send post-purchase emails to thank customers for their business and request feedback on their experience.

- Use this feedback to improve your products and services and build customer loyalty.

8. **<u>Automated Drip Campaigns</u>**:

- Set up automated drip campaigns that deliver a series of targeted emails based on specific triggers or actions.

- Drip campaigns can nurture leads, re-engage inactive customers, or upsell complementary products.

9. <u>**Monitoring Email Metrics:**</u>

- Track email open rates, click-through rates, conversion rates, and other key metrics to measure the effectiveness of your campaigns.

- Use this data to refine your email marketing strategy and optimize engagement.

10. <u>**Compliance with Email Regulations**</u>:

- Ensure compliance with email marketing regulations, such as obtaining proper consent from subscribers and including an easy opt-out option.

Email marketing and automation are valuable tools for engaging with your agrochemical customers throughout their journey. By delivering relevant and timely content, you can build lasting relationships, enhance customer loyalty, and drive sales for your agrochemical products. Remember to continuously analyze performance data and adapt your strategies to meet the changing needs of your audience.

Utilizing SEO and content marketing to reach a wider audience

Utilizing SEO (Search Engine Optimization) and content marketing in your marketing plan is a powerful combination that can significantly expand your reach and attract a wider audience to your agrochemical business. Here's an in-depth exploration of how SEO and content marketing work together to achieve these goals:

1. <u>**Understanding SEO and Content Marketing:**</u>

- SEO is the practice of optimizing your website and online content to rank higher in search engine results for relevant keywords and phrases.

- Content marketing involves creating and distributing valuable, relevant, and consistent content to attract and engage a target audience.

2. <u>**Keyword Research and Targeting**</u>:

- Conduct thorough keyword research to identify the most relevant and high-traffic keywords related to agrochemical products and the agricultural industry.

- Use these keywords strategically in your website content, blog posts, and other marketing materials to improve search engine visibility.

3. **<u>Creating High-Quality Content</u>**:

- Produce informative and valuable content that addresses the needs and interests of your target audience.

- Content can include blog articles, guides, infographics, videos, and more, catering to various preferences.

4. **<u>Optimizing On-Page Elements</u>**:

- Implement on-page SEO techniques, such as optimizing title tags, meta descriptions, heading tags, and URL structures.

- Ensure that your content is well-organized, easy to navigate, and optimized for both search engines and users.

5. **<u>Building Backlinks and Authority</u>**:

- Earn high-quality backlinks from reputable websites and publications within the agriculture and related industries.

- Backlinks enhance your website's authority and credibility in the eyes of search engines, leading to higher rankings.

6. **Promoting Content through Social Media**:

- Share your content on social media platforms to increase its visibility and attract more visitors to your website.

- Social media shares can also contribute to improved search engine rankings.

7. **Creating Evergreen and Long-Form Content**:

- Invest in creating evergreen content that remains relevant over time and provides long-term value to your audience.

- Long-form content, such as comprehensive guides or in-depth articles, tends to perform well in search engine rankings.

8. **<u>Monitoring Analytics and SEO Performance</u>**:

- Use analytics tools to track website traffic, keyword rankings, and user engagement with your content.

- Analyze data regularly to identify areas for improvement and capitalize on successful strategies.

9. **<u>Implementing Local SEO Strategies</u>**:

- For local agrochemical businesses, optimize for local search by including location-specific keywords and creating Google My Business profiles.

- Local SEO helps target customers in specific geographic regions.

10. **S<u>taying Updated with SEO Trends</u>**:

- SEO practices and algorithms evolve, so it's essential to stay updated with the latest trends and best practices.

- Adapt your content marketing and SEO strategies accordingly to maintain a competitive edge.

By incorporating SEO and content marketing into your marketing plan, you can improve your website's visibility in search engines, attract a wider audience, and establish your agrochemical business as a valuable resource within the agricultural community. As you continue to provide valuable content and optimize for relevant keywords, you'll strengthen your online presence and drive organic growth for your

business.

Chapter 7: Building Relationships with Distributors and Retailers

Selecting the right distribution partners

Selecting the right distribution partners for your agrochemical products in the Philippines is a critical step that can significantly impact the success of your business in the local market. Here's an in-depth exploration of key considerations to help you make informed decisions:

1. **Market Research and Understanding:**

- Conduct thorough market research to understand the agrochemical industry in the Philippines, including the demand for specific products, distribution channels, and competitive landscape.

- Identify potential distribution partners who have a deep understanding of the local market, its nuances, and the needs of Filipino farmers.

2. **Reputation and Credibility**:

- Seek out distribution partners with a strong reputation and credibility in the industry.

- Check their track record, customer feedback, and years of experience in distributing agrochemical products.

3. **Product Portfolio and Alignment**:

- Ensure that the distribution partner's product portfolio aligns with your agrochemical products.

- A complementary product mix can create cross-selling opportunities and a more robust market presence.

4. **<u>Geographic Coverage</u>**:

- - Assess the distribution partner's reach and coverage across the Philippines.

- - Consider partners with an extensive distribution network, especially in regions where your target customers are concentrated.

5. **<u>Logistics and Warehousing Capabilities</u>**:

- Evaluate the distribution partner's logistics capabilities, including storage, transportation, and inventory management.

- Efficient logistics can minimize delivery delays and ensure products reach customers promptly.

6. **<u>Financial Stability and Payment Terms</u>**:

- Verify the financial stability of potential distribution partners.

- Discuss payment terms, credit policies, and any other financial arrangements to ensure a mutually beneficial partnership.

7. **<u>Marketing and Sales Support</u>**:

- Inquire about the distribution partner's marketing and sales support capabilities.

- Partners who can promote and actively sell your agrochemical products will contribute to market penetration.

8. **<u>Compliance and Legal Aspects</u>**:

- Ensure the distribution partner complies with all local laws, regulations, and licensing requirements for agrochemical distribution.

- Review contracts carefully to safeguard your interests and clarify expectations.

9. **<u>Training and Technical Support:</u>**

- Consider partners who can provide technical training and support to customers using your products.

- Adequate training can enhance product knowledge and customer satisfaction.

10. **<u>Communication and Relationship Building</u>**:

- Establish open lines of communication with potential distribution partners.

- A strong and transparent relationship fosters collaboration and helps address any issues that may arise.

11. **<u>Flexibility and Adaptability</u>**:

- Look for distribution partners who can adapt to market changes and respond to emerging trends.

- Flexibility in adjusting strategies and approaches is crucial in the ever-evolving agrochemical industry.

Selecting the right distribution partners for your agrochemical products in the Philippines requires careful consideration and due diligence. Collaborating with reputable and reliable partners who understand the local market dynamics can pave the way for a successful market entry and long-term growth in the Philippine agriculture sector.

Training and supporting retailers

Training and supporting Filipino retailers of agrochemical products is a critical aspect of successful distribution and market penetration in the Philippines. By providing comprehensive training and ongoing support, you can empower retailers to effectively promote and sell your agrochemical products, enhance customer satisfaction, and build strong partnerships. Here's an in-depth exploration of key strategies for training and supporting Filipino retailers:

1. Product Knowledge Training:

- Conduct in-depth product knowledge training sessions for retailers, covering the features, benefits, and proper usage of your agrochemical products.

- Educate retailers about the specific crops and agricultural practices in the Philippines that can benefit from your products.

2. Safety and Regulatory Compliance:

- Emphasize safety protocols and compliance with local regulations regarding the handling, storage, and distribution of agrochemical products.

- Ensure that retailers understand the importance of responsible product usage and environmental stewardship.

3<u>. Technical Support and Troubleshooting:</u>

- Establish a dedicated technical support team to assist retailers with complex inquiries and troubleshooting.

- Provide clear channels of communication for retailers to seek assistance promptly.

4<u>. Sales Techniques and Selling Points:</u>

- Train retailers on effective sales techniques and the unique selling points of your agrochemical products.

- Equip them with persuasive arguments to communicate the value proposition to customers.

<u>5. Marketing and Promotional Support:</u>

- Offer marketing materials, such as brochures, posters, and product displays, to help retailers promote your agrochemical products effectively.

- Collaborate on joint promotional campaigns to increase brand visibility and drive sales.

6. Local Language and Cultural Sensitivity:

- Use local language and cultural nuances in training materials and support interactions to resonate with Filipino retailers.

- Demonstrate cultural sensitivity in all communications and engagements.

7. Customer Service Training:

- Train retailers on excellent customer service practices to enhance the overall shopping experience for customers.

- Encourage retailers to actively listen to customers' needs and offer personalized recommendations.

8. Regular Training Updates:

- Provide regular updates on product launches, improvements, and industry trends to keep retailers informed and engaged.

- Continuous learning helps retailers stay competitive and confident in promoting your products.

9. Sales Incentives and Rewards:

- Implement sales incentive programs to reward top-performing retailers for their efforts and achievements.

- Incentives can motivate retailers to go the extra mile in promoting and selling your agrochemical products.

10. Monitoring and Feedback Collection:

- Monitor retailer performance and collect feedback to identify areas for improvement.

- Conduct periodic surveys or interviews to understand retailers' challenges and suggestions.

11. Relationship Building and Collaboration:

- Foster a collaborative and supportive relationship with retailers, promoting open communication and mutual respect.

- Regularly engage with retailers to address their concerns and demonstrate your commitment to their success.

By investing in comprehensive training and ongoing support for Filipino retailers, you can create a network of knowledgeable and motivated partners who will play a vital role in effectively distributing and promoting your agrochemical products in the Philippine market. Empowered retailers can contribute significantly to market expansion, customer satisfaction, and the overall success of your business in the Philippines.

Implementing effective channel management strategies

Implementing effective channel management strategies for your agrochemical products is essential to ensure seamless distribution, maximize market reach, and maintain strong relationships with channel partners. Here's a comprehensive exploration of key strategies for successful channel management:

1. **Channel Selection and Evaluation**:
    - Evaluate different distribution channels available for agrochemical products, such as wholesalers, retailers, dealers, and e-commerce platforms.
    - Choose channels that align with your target market, product positioning, and overall business objectives.

2. **<u>Clearly Defined Channel Roles and Responsibilities:</u>**

- Clearly define the roles and responsibilities of each channel partner to avoid conflicts and ensure a smooth distribution process.

- Establish expectations regarding sales targets, inventory management, and promotional activities.

3. **<u>Channel Partner Training and Support</u>**:

- Provide comprehensive training and ongoing support to channel partners to enhance their product knowledge and sales skills.

- Offer technical assistance, marketing materials, and access to product information to facilitate their selling efforts.

4. **<u>Regular Communication and Collaboration</u>**:

- Maintain regular communication with channel partners to keep them informed about product updates, market trends, and promotional campaigns.

- Collaborate on joint marketing initiatives and coordinate efforts to drive sales collectively.

5. **Pricing and Margin Management:**

- Establish competitive pricing strategies that provide reasonable margins for channel partners while ensuring profitability for your agrochemical business.

- Regularly review and adjust pricing based on market dynamics and competition.

6. **Inventory and Supply Chain Management**:

- Optimize inventory management to avoid stockouts and excess inventory in the channel.

- Work closely with channel partners to ensure a smooth and efficient supply chain process.

7. Channel Performance Evaluation:

- Implement performance metrics to assess the effectiveness of each channel and individual partners.

- Analyze sales data, customer feedback, and other relevant metrics to identify areas for improvement.

8. Channel Partner Incentives and Rewards:

- Offer incentives and rewards to top-performing channel partners as a way to motivate them and foster loyalty.

- Incentive programs can be based on sales achievements, market expansion, or other key performance indicators.

9. **<u>Resolving Channel Conflicts</u>**:

- Address and resolve channel conflicts promptly and diplomatically to maintain healthy working relationships.

- Open communication and mediation can help prevent conflicts from escalating.

10. **<u>Market Development and Expansion</u>**:

- Collaborate with channel partners to identify new market opportunities and potential areas for expansion.

- Together, explore untapped segments and geographies to grow market share.

11. **<u>Feedback Collection and Implementation</u>**:

- Actively seek feedback from channel partners on their challenges, needs, and suggestions for improvement.

- Implement changes based on feedback to enhance the overall channel management process.

By implementing effective channel management strategies, you can optimize the performance of your distribution channels, strengthen partnerships with channel partners, and drive the success of your agrochemical products in the market. Flexibility, communication, and a customer-centric approach are essential in adapting to market changes and maintaining a competitive edge in the agrochemical industry.

Chapter 8: Promotional Activities and Campaigns

Designing impactful promotional campaigns

Designing impactful promotional campaigns for your agrochemical products that are uniquely Filipino requires a deep understanding of the local culture, agricultural practices, and consumer preferences. By incorporating elements that resonate with the Filipino audience, you can create campaigns that are both effective and culturally relevant. Here's an in-depth exploration of key strategies to achieve this:

1. Showcasing Local Farmers and Agriculture:

- Feature Filipino farmers in your promotional campaigns to humanize the brand and connect with the audience emotionally.

- Highlight the importance of agriculture in the Philippines and how your agrochemical products contribute to improving yields and livelihoods.

2. Celebrating Festivals and Traditions:

- Align your promotional campaigns with significant Filipino festivals and agricultural traditions.

- Incorporate festive imagery, colors, and themes that reflect the spirit of these celebrations.

3. Using Local Language and Slang:

- Use local language and slang in your campaign messages to create a sense of familiarity and relatability.

- Speak directly to the Filipino audience in a way that resonates with their daily conversations.

4<u>. Highlighting Filipino Crops and Agriculture Practices:</u>

- Focus on crops that are important to the Philippine agriculture industry, such as rice, corn, coconut, and various fruits and vegetables.

- Illustrate how your agrochemical products can enhance the growth and quality of these crops.

5<u>. Emphasizing Sustainability and Environmental Impact:</u>

- Appeal to the Filipino culture's strong sense of environmental stewardship by highlighting the sustainability and eco-friendly aspects of your products.

- Showcase how your agrochemical solutions contribute to preserving the environment and conserving natural resources.

6. Incorporating Local Symbols and Icons:

- Integrate Filipino symbols, national icons, or agricultural elements unique to the Philippines into your campaign visuals.

- This fosters a sense of pride and ownership among the Filipino audience.

7. Engaging in Community Initiatives:

- Sponsor or participate in local community initiatives related to agriculture, education, or environmental conservation.

- Engaging in community-based projects demonstrates your commitment to the welfare of Filipino farmers and communities.

8. Utilizing Social Media and Influencers:

- Leverage the popularity of social media in the Philippines to reach a wider audience.

- Collaborate with local influencers, especially those with ties to agriculture or rural communities, to amplify your campaign's reach.

9. Offering Filipino-Themed Promotions and Rewards:

- Design promotions, discounts, or rewards that align with Filipino cultural themes and preferences.

- For example, offer "harvest season" discounts or rewards tied to local festivals.

10. Storytelling and Testimonials:

- Use storytelling to share success stories and testimonials from Filipino farmers who have benefitted from using your agrochemical products.

- Authentic stories resonate deeply with the Filipino audience and build trust in your brand.

By designing promotional campaigns that are uniquely Filipino, you can create a strong emotional connection with the local audience and establish your agrochemical brand as a partner that understands and supports the needs of Filipino farmers. Remember to stay authentic, culturally sensitive, and socially responsible in your campaigns to foster lasting relationships with the Filipino market.

Organizing product demonstrations and field days

Organizing product demonstrations and field days for agrochemical products is a highly effective way to showcase the benefits and effectiveness of your products to potential customers, farmers, and agribusiness stakeholders. These events provide a hands-on experience, allowing participants to see the products in action and gain valuable insights. Here's an in-depth exploration of the benefits and key considerations for organizing such events:

Benefits of Product Demonstrations and Field Days:

1. **Interactive Learning Experience:**

- Product demonstrations and field days offer an interactive and practical learning experience for attendees.

- Participants can see the actual application of agrochemical products and understand their impact on crops and agricultural practices.

2. **Enhanced Product Understanding**:

- Demonstrations allow farmers and stakeholders to better understand how your agrochemical products work and how they address specific agricultural challenges.

- Seeing the products in action builds confidence in their efficacy.

3. **Building Trust and Credibility**:

- Hands-on experiences create a sense of trust and credibility, as participants witness the actual results of your products.

- Demonstrating transparency and expertise further strengthens your brand's reputation.

4. **<u>Networking and Relationship Building</u>**:

- Product demonstrations and field days provide an excellent opportunity to network with potential customers, industry experts, and key stakeholders.

- Building personal relationships can lead to long-term partnerships and word-of-mouth referrals.

5. **<u>Collecting Feedback and Insights</u>**:

- Interacting directly with attendees allows you to collect valuable feedback and insights on your products' performance.

- Feedback helps you make improvements and address concerns proactively.

6. **<u>Showcasing Innovation and Technology</u>**:

- Field days can serve as a platform to showcase the innovation and technology behind your agrochemical products.

- Highlighting the scientific aspects can appeal to a tech-savvy audience.

Key Considerations for Organizing Product Demonstrations and Field Days:

1. <u>Venue Selection:</u>

- Choose a suitable venue with adequate space to accommodate participants, product displays, and demonstration areas.

- Consider accessibility and proximity to the target audience, such as farms or agricultural communities.

2. Invitations and Outreach:

- Send out invitations to potential customers, farmers, distributors, agribusinesses, and relevant industry stakeholders.

- Utilize various communication channels, such as email, social media, and local community networks, to promote the event.

3. Expert Demonstrators and Presenters:

- Ensure you have expert demonstrators and presenters who can effectively communicate the features and benefits of your products.

- Knowledgeable personnel can answer questions and provide valuable insights to attendees.

4. Event Agenda and Activities:

- Plan a well-structured agenda that includes product demonstrations, presentations, Q&A sessions, and networking opportunities.

- Incorporate hands-on activities and interactive sessions to keep participants engaged.

5. Safety Measures:

- Adhere to safety protocols and guidelines during product demonstrations to ensure the well-being of attendees and the environment.

- Clearly communicate safety instructions to all participants.

6. Promotional Materials and Giveaways:

- Prepare promotional materials, brochures, and samples to distribute to attendees.

- Consider offering promotional giveaways to create a positive impression and encourage future engagement.

7. Post-Event Follow-up:

- Follow up with attendees after the event to thank them for their participation and gather additional feedback.

- Maintain communication to nurture potential leads and build long-term relationships.

Product demonstrations and field days are valuable opportunities to engage with your target audience, demonstrate the effectiveness of your agrochemical products, and foster positive relationships with farmers and stakeholders. By carefully planning and executing these events, you can create lasting impressions and drive business growth in the agricultural market.

Sponsorships, events, and trade shows for brand exposure:

Sponsorships, events, and trade shows are powerful marketing tools that can significantly enhance brand exposure for agrochemical products. By strategically participating in or sponsoring relevant events and trade shows, you can reach a broader audience, engage with key industry stakeholders, and position your brand as a leading authority in the agrochemical sector. Here's an in-depth exploration of the benefits and considerations for utilizing these marketing avenues:

Benefits of Sponsorships, Events, and Trade Shows:

1. Increased Brand Visibility:

   - Sponsoring or participating in high-profile events and trade shows allows your agrochemical brand to gain exposure to a wide audience, including potential customers, distributors, and industry professionals.

   - Your brand name and products become associated with the event, increasing its visibility and reach.

2. Targeted Audience Engagement:

   - Events and trade shows provide access to a targeted audience of farmers, agribusiness professionals, and decision-makers in the agriculture industry.

   - You can engage directly with this audience, showcasing your products and addressing their specific needs and inquiries.

3. Networking and Partnerships:

   - Participation in industry events and trade shows creates networking opportunities with other agrochemical companies, distributors, and potential business partners.

- Building relationships with industry stakeholders can lead to collaboration and expansion opportunities.

4. Product Demonstrations and Launches:

- Trade shows and sponsored events offer a platform for live product demonstrations and launches.

- Attendees can experience your agrochemical products firsthand, gaining confidence in their effectiveness.

5. Industry Thought Leadership:

- Active involvement in industry events and sponsorships helps establish your brand as a thought leader in the agrochemical sector.

- Sharing knowledge and insights during seminars or panel discussions positions your brand as an authority in the field.

6. Market Research and Customer Feedback:

- Events and trade shows offer opportunities to gather market research and customer feedback.

- Engaging with attendees allows you to understand market trends, preferences, and challenges better.

7. Competitor Analysis:

- Participating in industry events provides insight into competitors' products, strategies, and market positioning.

- Understanding competitor offerings can help you refine your own marketing approach.

Considerations for Sponsorships, Events, and Trade Shows:

<u>1. Relevance and Alignment:</u>

- Choose events and sponsorships that align with your agrochemical products and target audience.

- Ensure the event's theme and audience match your marketing objectives.

2. Budget and ROI Analysis:

   - Evaluate the cost-benefit ratio of each sponsorship or event opportunity.

   - Consider the potential return on investment in terms of brand exposure, lead generation, and long-term business impact.

3. Preparation and Logistics:

   - Plan and prepare well in advance for events and trade shows to ensure smooth execution.

   - Coordinate logistics, staffing, and promotional materials to create a positive brand experience.

4. Engaging Booth Design:

- Design an attractive and engaging booth that effectively showcases your agrochemical products.

- Incorporate visuals, product samples, and interactive elements to draw attendees' attention.

5. Post-Event Follow-up:

- Follow up with leads and contacts generated during events and trade shows.

- Maintain communication to nurture relationships and convert leads into customers.

6. Measuring Success:

- Define key performance indicators (KPIs) to measure the success of sponsorships and event participation.

- Track metrics such as lead generation, customer conversions, and brand reach.

By strategically leveraging sponsorships, events, and trade shows, your agrochemical brand can gain significant exposure, establish authority in the industry, and cultivate valuable relationships with stakeholders. Careful planning, alignment with marketing goals, and post-event follow-up are essential to making the most of these marketing opportunities for long-term business growth.

Chapter 9: Customer Relationship Management (CRM)

Error! Filename not specified.

Implementing CRM systems for better customer retention

Implementing Customer Relationship Management (CRM) systems for better Filipino customer retention of your agrochemical products can significantly enhance customer satisfaction, loyalty, and overall business success. CRM systems are valuable tools that help you manage interactions with customers, gather valuable data, and provide personalized experiences. Here's an in-depth exploration of the benefits and strategies for implementing CRM systems in the context of the Filipino market:

Benefits of CRM Systems for Agrochemical Customer Retention:

1. Data Centralization and Organization:

  - CRM systems centralize customer data, including contact information, purchase history, preferences, and interactions.

  - Having a unified view of each customer helps you understand their needs and offer personalized support.

2. Improved Customer Communication:

  - CRM systems enable more effective and timely communication with Filipino customers.

  - You can send personalized messages, product updates, and promotional offers based on individual preferences.

3. Enhanced Customer Service:

- CRM systems allow you to track customer inquiries, complaints, and requests, enabling prompt and efficient resolution.

- Timely and satisfactory responses build trust and loyalty.

4. Targeted Marketing and Segmentation:

- Segmenting Filipino customers based on their behavior and preferences allows you to deliver targeted marketing campaigns.

- Tailored promotions and content increase the likelihood of engagement and repeat purchases.

5. Customer Feedback and Satisfaction Tracking:

- CRM systems facilitate the collection of customer feedback and satisfaction ratings.

- Understanding customer sentiment helps you identify areas for improvement and measure the success of retention strategies.

6. Personalization and Customer Retention Strategies:

- Utilize CRM data to create personalized offers, loyalty programs, and incentives for Filipino customers.

- Personalized experiences foster a sense of appreciation and strengthen customer loyalty.

7. Sales and Upselling Opportunities:

- CRM systems provide insights into customer buying patterns and preferences.

- This data can identify upselling opportunities and encourage customers to try new or complementary agrochemical products.

Strategies for Implementing CRM Systems in the Filipino Market:

1. Selecting the Right CRM Platform:

 - Choose a CRM platform that aligns with the specific needs and size of your agrochemical business.

 - Consider cloud-based solutions for accessibility and scalability.

2. Data Migration and Integration:

 - Ensure seamless data migration from existing systems to the new CRM platform.

 - Integrate CRM with other business tools, such as marketing automation and inventory management systems.

3. Training and User Adoption:

- Provide comprehensive training to your team on using the CRM system effectively.

- Encourage user adoption and emphasize the benefits of the CRM system for customer retention.

4. Customer Data Privacy and Compliance:

- Comply with data privacy regulations in the Philippines, such as the Data Privacy Act of 2012.

- Safeguard customer data and seek consent for its usage.

5. Automating Customer Interactions:

- Implement automation features in the CRM system for email marketing, follow-ups, and customer support.

- Automation streamlines processes and ensures timely customer engagement.

6. Analyzing Customer Behavior:

- Use CRM analytics to gain insights into customer behavior, preferences, and retention patterns.

- Use this data to tailor marketing and retention strategies accordingly.

7. Continuous Improvement:

- Continuously analyze CRM data and customer feedback to identify areas for improvement in products, services, and customer interactions.

- Use feedback to enhance customer experiences and drive better retention rates.

By implementing CRM systems tailored to the Filipino market, your agrochemical business can build lasting relationships with customers, enhance customer retention, and drive customer loyalty. The ability to offer personalized experiences, targeted marketing, and excellent customer service will contribute to long-term success and growth in the Philippine agriculture sector.

Personalization and customer support

Personalization and customer support are essential elements for agrochemical products that can significantly enhance customer satisfaction, loyalty, and overall business success. Providing personalized experiences and exceptional customer support demonstrates a genuine commitment to meeting the unique needs of customers in the agricultural industry. Here's an in-depth exploration of the benefits and strategies for implementing personalization and customer support for agrochemical products:

Benefits of Personalization and Customer Support:

1. Enhanced Customer Satisfaction:

   - Personalized experiences and tailored support make customers feel valued and understood.

   - Meeting their specific needs and preferences leads to higher satisfaction levels.

2. Improved Customer Loyalty and Retention:

   - When customers receive personalized attention and excellent support, they are more likely to remain loyal to your agrochemical brand.

   - Repeat business and long-term relationships contribute to higher customer retention rates.

3. Increased Customer Engagement:

   - Personalization captures customers' attention and encourages active engagement with your agrochemical products and brand.

- Engaged customers are more likely to participate in promotions, provide feedback, and advocate for your brand.

4. Effective Marketing and Communication:

  - Personalized communication allows you to deliver relevant and targeted messages to specific customer segments.

  - Tailored marketing campaigns improve the effectiveness of your promotional efforts.

5. Positive Word-of-Mouth and Reputation:

  - Satisfied customers who receive personalized support are more likely to share positive experiences with others.

  - Positive word-of-mouth enhances your brand reputation and attracts new customers.

Strategies for Personalization and Customer Support:

1. Customer Profiling and Segmentation:

   - Segment customers based on factors such as their crop type, location, purchase history, and preferences.

   - Develop personalized offers, content, and marketing campaigns for each segment.

2. Personalized Recommendations:

   - Use customer data and behavior to provide personalized product recommendations that align with their needs.

   - Recommend agrochemical products that complement their existing purchases.

3. Tailored Marketing Content:

   - Customize marketing content, such as emails, newsletters, and social media posts, to address the specific interests of different customer segments.

- Offer valuable insights and educational content related to their crops and agricultural practices.

4. Responsive Customer Support:

   - Ensure prompt and responsive customer support through multiple channels, such as phone, email, and social media.

   - Address customer inquiries, complaints, and requests in a timely and professional manner.

5. Product Training and Resources:

   - Provide training resources and materials to customers to maximize the effectiveness of your agrochemical products.

   - Offer guides, videos, and workshops to educate customers on proper product usage.

6. Proactive Support and Follow-Up:

- Proactively reach out to customers to check their satisfaction after product purchases or applications.

- Offer assistance, collect feedback, and address any concerns promptly.

7. Loyalty Programs and Incentives:

- Implement loyalty programs that reward customers for repeat purchases and engagement.

- Offer incentives, discounts, or exclusive access to new products for loyal customers.

8. Data Privacy and Consent:

- Respect customer data privacy and seek consent for personalized marketing and support efforts.

- Comply with data protection regulations in the country of operation.

By embracing personalization and providing exceptional customer support, your agrochemical business can build strong customer relationships, foster loyalty, and establish a reputation as a customer-centric brand. Investing in personalization and support not only benefits individual customers but also contributes to the long-term success and growth of your agrochemical products in the market.

Gathering feedback and addressing concerns

Gathering feedback and addressing concerns of Filipino agrochemical product users is a crucial aspect of maintaining customer satisfaction and continuously improving your products and services. By actively seeking and addressing feedback, you can build trust with your customers, identify areas for improvement, and tailor your offerings to better meet their needs. Here's an in-depth exploration of the importance and strategies for gathering feedback and addressing concerns of Filipino agrochemical product users:

Importance of Gathering Feedback and Addressing Concerns:

1. Customer Satisfaction and Loyalty:

   - Listening to customer feedback and addressing their concerns demonstrates that you value their opinions and are committed to their satisfaction.

   - Satisfied customers are more likely to remain loyal to your agrochemical brand and recommend your products to others.

2. Quality Improvement:

   - Feedback provides valuable insights into the performance and effectiveness of your agrochemical products.

   - Identifying areas for improvement helps you enhance product quality and optimize formulations.

3. Market Insights and Trends:

  - Customer feedback offers valuable market insights and helps you understand the evolving needs and trends in the Filipino agricultural industry.

  - These insights can guide product development and marketing strategies.

4. Brand Reputation and Trust:

  - Promptly addressing customer concerns builds a positive brand reputation and fosters trust with your customer base.

  - Transparent and effective communication during challenging situations enhances brand credibility.

5. Customer Retention and Repeat Business:

- Resolving customer concerns and providing satisfactory solutions contribute to customer retention and repeat business.

- Customers are more likely to return if they have positive experiences with your support team.

Strategies for Gathering Feedback and Addressing Concerns:

1. Customer Surveys and Questionnaires:

- Conduct regular customer surveys and questionnaires to gather structured feedback on product performance, customer service, and overall satisfaction.

- Use both online and offline survey methods for broader reach.

2. Social Media Monitoring:

- Monitor social media channels for customer feedback, comments, and concerns related to your agrochemical products.

- Respond promptly and professionally to address any issues raised.

3. Customer Support Channels:

- Maintain accessible and responsive customer support channels, such as phone, email, and live chat.

- Train support staff to handle inquiries and concerns effectively.

4. Feedback Forms at Events:

- Distribute feedback forms during product demonstrations, field days, and other events.

- Encourage participants to share their thoughts and experiences.

5. Focus Group Discussions:

   - Organize focus group discussions with a diverse group of Filipino farmers to gain in-depth insights into their needs and preferences.

   - Use the findings to inform product development and marketing strategies.

6. Personalized Follow-Ups:

   - Follow up with customers after product purchases to gather their feedback and check their satisfaction.

   - Address any concerns or issues raised during these interactions.

7. Product Testing Programs:

   - Invite select customers to participate in product testing programs.

- Their feedback can be invaluable in refining product formulations.

8. Online Review Monitoring:

  - Monitor online reviews and ratings of your agrochemical products on e-commerce platforms and review websites.

  - Respond to reviews, both positive and negative, to engage with customers and address concerns.

By actively seeking and addressing feedback from Filipino agrochemical product users, you demonstrate a customer-centric approach and a commitment to continuous improvement. Utilize the insights gained to make data-driven decisions, enhance product offerings, and provide exceptional customer support. Listening to your customers and acting on their feedback will strengthen your brand's position in the market and contribute to long-term success in the Filipino agricultural industry.

Chapter 10: Sustainability and Responsible Marketing

Error! Filename not specified.

Embracing sustainability practices in agrochemical marketing

Embracing sustainability practices in agrochemical marketing is essential for the long-term success of both your business and the agricultural industry as a whole. By promoting sustainable agricultural practices and highlighting the eco-friendly aspects of your agrochemical products, you can build a positive brand image, meet evolving consumer expectations, and contribute to environmental conservation. Here's an in-depth exploration of the benefits and strategies for integrating sustainability practices into agrochemical marketing:

Benefits of Embracing Sustainability Practices:

1. Positive Brand Image:

   - Demonstrating a commitment to sustainability enhances your brand's reputation and fosters positive perceptions among consumers and stakeholders.

   - Consumers are increasingly choosing products from companies that prioritize environmental responsibility.

2. Market Differentiation:

   - Sustainability-focused marketing sets your agrochemical products apart from competitors, creating a unique selling proposition in the market.

   - Highlighting eco-friendly aspects can attract environmentally conscious customers.

3. Customer Loyalty and Engagement:

- Customers who align with sustainable values are more likely to be loyal to your brand and actively engage with your marketing initiatives.

   - Sustainable practices can foster a sense of shared responsibility and connection with your agrochemical brand.

4. Compliance with Regulations:

   - Embracing sustainability practices helps your business comply with increasingly stringent environmental regulations.

   - Meeting regulatory requirements can prevent legal issues and safeguard your brand reputation.

5. Long-Term Viability:

   - Sustainable practices contribute to the long-term viability of the agricultural industry by conserving natural resources and preserving ecosystems.

- Protecting the environment ensures the availability of resources for future generations.

Strategies for Integrating Sustainability into Agrochemical Marketing

1. Communicate Eco-Friendly Features:

   - Clearly communicate the eco-friendly features and benefits of your agrochemical products in marketing materials and campaigns.

   - Highlight aspects such as reduced environmental impact, low toxicity, and biodegradability.

2. Promote Responsible Use and Practices:

   - Educate farmers on responsible agrochemical usage, proper application techniques, and safety measures.

- Provide guidelines for minimizing waste and pollution during product application.

3. Certifications and Labels:

- Obtain relevant certifications and eco-labels that demonstrate your commitment to sustainability.

- Display these certifications on product packaging and marketing materials to build trust.

4. Support Sustainable Farming Techniques:

- Promote and support sustainable farming techniques, such as integrated pest management and organic farming.

- Position your agrochemical products as solutions that complement these practices.

5. Transparency and Traceability:

- Be transparent about the environmental impact of your agrochemical products and manufacturing processes.

- Provide information on sourcing, production, and the life cycle of your products.

6. Collaborate with Sustainable Initiatives:

- Partner with sustainable agriculture initiatives, NGOs, or local communities to show your commitment to environmental conservation.

- Participate in projects that promote sustainable farming and ecological preservation.

7. Sustainability Reporting:

- Publish sustainability reports that outline your efforts, progress, and future sustainability goals.

- Share these reports with customers and stakeholders to reinforce your dedication to sustainability.

8. Engage in Social Responsibility:

- Demonstrate social responsibility by investing in community projects, education, or environmental restoration initiatives.

- Engaging in socially impactful projects strengthens your brand's reputation.

By integrating sustainability practices into your agrochemical marketing, you can create a positive impact on the environment, society, and the agricultural industry. Embracing sustainability not only benefits your brand but also contributes to the larger goal of building a more sustainable and resilient agricultural sector for future generations.

Communicating environmental benefits responsibly

Communicating the environmental benefits of agrochemicals responsibly is crucial to ensure transparency, build trust with customers, and promote sustainable agriculture practices. While agrochemicals can offer environmental advantages when used correctly, it's essential to present the information accurately and avoid misleading claims. Here's an in-depth exploration of strategies for responsible communication of the environmental benefits of agrochemicals:

1. Accurate Information Sharing:

  - Share factual and evidence-based information on the environmental benefits of agrochemicals.

  - Provide data from reputable sources, studies, and research to back up your claims.

2. Clear and Transparent Messaging:

- Clearly communicate the specific environmental benefits of your agrochemical products without exaggeration or vague language.

- Avoid making broad claims that cannot be substantiated.

3. Emphasize Responsible Usage:

- Clearly state that the environmental benefits are contingent upon proper and responsible usage of agrochemical products.

- Provide guidelines and best practices for safe and effective application.

4. Use Real-World Examples:

- Share real-world examples of how agrochemicals have positively impacted the environment when used responsibly.

- Highlight success stories and case studies of farmers who have achieved sustainable outcomes.

5. Disclose Limitations and Risks

   - Be transparent about the limitations and potential risks of agrochemical usage.

   - Acknowledge any adverse effects that might occur if products are not used correctly.

6. Educate Farmers and Users

   - Provide educational materials and training to farmers and users on the environmental benefits and responsible use of agrochemicals.

   - Empower them with knowledge to make informed decisions.

7. Avoid Greenwashing

- Do not engage in "greenwashing," which involves making misleading or unsubstantiated claims about the environmental benefits of products.

  - Be honest about the potential impacts, both positive and negative.

8. Use Labels and Certifications

  - Use recognized eco-labels and certifications that validate the environmental benefits of your agrochemical products.

  - Ensure that the labels are accurate and up-to-date.

9. Collaborate with Third Parties

  - Work with independent organizations or experts to verify the environmental benefits of your agrochemical products.

  - External validation adds credibility to your claims.

10. Regular Monitoring and Reporting

- Continuously monitor the environmental impact of your agrochemical products and report the findings regularly.

- Share the results, both positive and negative, with stakeholders.

11. Promote Integrated Pest Management (IPM

- Emphasize the role of agrochemicals as one component of an Integrated Pest Management (IPM) approach.

- IPM advocates for a holistic and sustainable approach to pest and disease management.

Responsible communication of the environmental benefits of agrochemicals is essential to build trust among consumers, farmers, and stakeholders. By presenting accurate and transparent information, supporting responsible usage, and promoting sustainable agricultural practices, your agrochemical business can contribute to the conservation of the environment while meeting the needs of the agricultural industry.

Addressing safety and regulatory considerations:

Addressing safety and Philippine regulatory considerations for agrochemical products is vital to ensure the well-being of users, protect the environment, and comply with local laws and regulations. The Philippine government has established guidelines and regulations to safeguard public health, agricultural practices, and the environment from potential risks associated with agrochemicals. Here's an in-depth exploration of strategies for addressing safety and regulatory considerations for agrochemical products in the Philippines:

1. Product Registration and Compliance

- Before marketing and selling agrochemical products in the Philippines, ensure that they are registered with the appropriate regulatory authorities, such as the Fertilizer and Pesticide Authority (FPA) under the Department of Agriculture (DA).

- Comply with the requirements set forth in the Republic Act 9168 or the "Fertilizer and Pesticide Authority Act."

2. Labeling and Safety Data Sheets (SDS

- Ensure that agrochemical product labels include all necessary information, such as product name, active ingredients, usage instructions, precautions, and safety warnings.

- Provide Safety Data Sheets (SDS) to users, containing detailed information on product composition, hazards, handling, storage, and emergency procedures.

3. Proper Usage Guidelines

   - Educate farmers, distributors, and users about proper agrochemical usage, application rates, safety precautions, and environmental protection measures.

   - Promote Integrated Pest Management (IPM) practices to reduce the reliance on agrochemicals.

4. Training and Education Programs

   - Conduct training and educational programs for farmers and users to enhance their understanding of agrochemical safety and responsible application techniques.

   - Collaborate with local agricultural extension offices and NGOs to reach a broader audience.

5. Monitoring and Surveillance

- Regularly monitor and assess the safety and environmental impact of agrochemical products through field trials and studies.

- Share the findings with regulatory authorities and the public.

6. Emergency Response Plans

- Develop and communicate emergency response plans to handle accidents, spills, or incidents related to agrochemical usage.

- Train employees and stakeholders on appropriate emergency procedures.

7. Compliance with Hazardous Substances Regulations

- Comply with the Department of Environment and Natural Resources (DENR) regulations concerning hazardous substances.

- Properly manage and dispose of hazardous waste generated during agrochemical manufacturing, distribution, and use.

8. Public Awareness Campaigns

  - Participate in public awareness campaigns to promote safe agrochemical practices and environmental protection.

  - Collaborate with government agencies and NGOs to amplify the message.

9. Regular Updates on Regulations

  - Stay informed about changes or updates in agrochemical regulations in the Philippines.

  - Ensure that your products and practices remain compliant with the latest requirements.

10. Collaboration with Local Authorities

- Work closely with local agricultural and environmental authorities to address safety concerns and ensure responsible agrochemical use.

  - Engage in discussions and cooperation to improve industry practices.

Addressing safety and regulatory considerations for agrochemical products is not only a legal obligation but also an ethical responsibility. By prioritizing the safety of users, protecting the environment, and complying with Philippine regulations, your agrochemical business can build a positive reputation, gain public trust, and contribute to sustainable agricultural practices in the country.

Chapter 11: Measuring Marketing Effectiveness

Error! Filename not specified.

Key performance indicators (KPIs) for agrochemical marketing

Key Performance Indicators (KPIs) are essential metrics that help agrochemical companies measure the success and effectiveness of their marketing efforts. By tracking these KPIs, businesses can gain valuable insights into the performance of their marketing strategies and make data-driven decisions to optimize their campaigns. Here are some key performance indicators for agrochemical marketing:

1. **Sales Revenue**: The total revenue generated from agrochemical product sales is a fundamental KPI. It directly reflects the effectiveness of marketing efforts in driving product demand and sales.

2. **Return on Investment (ROI):** This metric measures the return on marketing investment. It compares the revenue generated from marketing efforts against the total marketing

costs, providing insights into the overall profitability of marketing campaigns.

3. **Customer Acquisition Cost (CAC**): CAC calculates the average cost of acquiring a new customer. It helps assess the efficiency of marketing channels and the cost-effectiveness of acquiring new customers.

4. **Customer Retention Rate:** This KPI measures the percentage of customers who continue to purchase agrochemical products over a specific period. A high customer retention rate indicates customer satisfaction and loyalty.

5. **Customer Lifetime Value (CLV):** CLV calculates the total revenue generated from a customer over their entire relationship with the business. Understanding CLV helps

prioritize customer retention strategies and customer support efforts.

6. **Lead Conversion Rate:** This metric tracks the percentage of leads that convert into paying customers. A higher lead conversion rate indicates the effectiveness of lead generation and sales efforts.

7. **Website Traffic and Engagement:** Monitoring website traffic, page views, and average session duration helps gauge the effectiveness of online marketing efforts. Higher traffic and engagement reflect successful website promotion.

8. **Conversion Rate:** The conversion rate measures the percentage of website visitors who take a desired action, such as signing up for newsletters or making a purchase. A higher

conversion rate indicates effective website design and compelling calls-to-action.

9. **Social Media Engagement:** Tracking likes, shares, comments, and click-through rates on social media posts helps evaluate the impact of social media marketing on audience engagement and brand visibility.

10. **Brand Awareness and Recognition:** Conducting brand awareness surveys and monitoring brand mentions on social media and other platforms provides insights into the effectiveness of brand-building efforts.

11. **Email Marketing Metrics**: Open rates, click-through rates, and email subscription growth help measure the success of email marketing campaigns in engaging and retaining customers.

12. **Market Share**: Tracking the percentage of market share that your agrochemical products hold in comparison to competitors helps assess your brand's position in the market.

13. **Customer Feedback and Reviews**: Monitoring customer feedback and online reviews helps gauge customer satisfaction and identify areas for improvement in products and customer service.

14. **Marketing Campaign Performance**: Evaluating the performance of specific marketing campaigns, such as product launches or seasonal promotions, helps optimize future marketing initiatives.

15. **Sustainability Impact**: If sustainability is a key focus in marketing efforts, measuring the impact of eco-friendly

products and sustainable practices on the environment can provide insights into the effectiveness of sustainability messaging.

Choosing the right KPIs depends on the specific marketing objectives and strategies of each agrochemical business. Regularly tracking and analyzing these KPIs can guide marketing decisions, refine strategies, and ensure successful outcomes in the competitive agrochemical market.

Analyzing marketing data and making data-driven decisions

Analyzing marketing data and making data-driven decisions is a crucial process for marketing agrochemical products effectively. In the modern digital age, data is abundant, and harnessing its insights empowers agrochemical companies to understand their customers, optimize marketing strategies, and maximize return on investment (ROI). Here's an in-depth exploration of the process of analyzing marketing data and the benefits of making data-driven decisions for marketing agrochemical products:

1. **<u>Data Collection and Consolidation</u>**:

   - Gather data from various sources, including website analytics, social media platforms, customer databases, email campaigns, and sales records.

   - Consolidate the data into a unified database or marketing analytics platform.

2. **<u>Define Key Performance Indicators (KPIs)</u>**:

   - Determine the specific KPIs that align with the marketing objectives of promoting agrochemical products.

   - Common KPIs may include sales revenue, customer acquisition cost, conversion rates, and website traffic.

3. **<u>Data Analysis and Visualization</u>**:

 - Analyze the marketing data to uncover patterns, trends, and correlations.

 - Use data visualization tools to present insights in easy-to-understand formats like graphs and charts.

4. **<u>Customer Segmentation and Profiling</u>**:

 - Segment customers based on factors like location, crop type, purchasing behavior, and engagement levels.

 - Create customer profiles to understand their preferences and needs.

5. **<u>Assess Marketing Campaign Performance</u>**:

 - Evaluate the performance of different marketing campaigns, such as email marketing, social media promotions, and content marketing.

- Identify which campaigns drove the most significant impact and return on investment.

6. **<u>Optimize Marketing Strategies</u>**:

  - Use data insights to optimize marketing strategies and allocate resources to the most effective channels and campaigns.

  - Adjust marketing messages, target audiences, and promotional timing based on data analysis.

7. **<u>Measure Customer Engagement:</u>**

  - Track customer engagement metrics, such as click-through rates, time spent on website pages, and social media interactions.

  - Analyze engagement data to identify areas for improvement and content optimization.

8. **A/B Testing and Experimentation**

   - Conduct A/B testing to compare the effectiveness of different marketing elements, such as email subject lines, website layouts, or ad copies.

   - Use data to determine which variations perform better and make data-driven decisions.

9. Personalization and Targeting:

   - Leverage customer data to personalize marketing messages and target specific customer segments with relevant offers.

   - Personalization increases the likelihood of customer engagement and conversion.

10. Continuous Improvement and Iteration:

   - Continuously analyze marketing data and make data-driven decisions based on real-time insights.

- Embrace an iterative approach to marketing, making improvements based on the latest data trends.

Benefits of Data-Driven Marketing Decisions

1. <u>Better Customer Understanding:</u> Data-driven decisions provide deeper insights into customer behavior, preferences, and pain points, leading to more effective marketing strategies.

2. <u>Improved ROI</u>: By optimizing marketing efforts based on data analysis, agrochemical companies can achieve higher returns on their marketing investments.

3. <u>Increased Customer Engagement</u>: Personalized and targeted marketing messages based on data analysis result in higher customer engagement and conversion rates.

4. <u>Optimized Content and Messaging</u>: Data-driven decisions help identify the most resonant content and messaging, ensuring that marketing efforts align with customer needs.

5. <u>Competitive Advantage:</u> Leveraging marketing data gives agrochemical companies a competitive edge by staying ahead of market trends and consumer demands.

In conclusion, analyzing marketing data and making data-driven decisions is essential for marketing agrochemical products successfully. The process enables agrochemical companies to understand their customers, refine marketing strategies, and deliver personalized, targeted, and impactful marketing campaigns that drive positive outcomes for both the business and its customers.

Continuous improvement and optimization

Continuous improvement and optimization of agrochemical marketing effectiveness is an ongoing process that involves refining marketing strategies, analyzing performance data, and adapting to changes in the market and customer preferences. By embracing a culture of continuous improvement, agrochemical companies can stay competitive, enhance customer engagement, and achieve better results from their marketing efforts. Here's an in-depth exploration of the importance and strategies for continuously improving and optimizing agrochemical marketing effectiveness:

Importance of Continuous Improvement in Agrochemical Marketing:

1. <u>Staying Relevant and Competitive</u>: The agricultural industry is dynamic, with changing trends, technologies, and customer preferences. Continuous improvement ensures that marketing strategies remain relevant and competitive.

2. <u>Adapting to Customer Needs:</u> Customer needs and expectations evolve over time. Continuous improvement allows agrochemical companies to adjust marketing approaches to meet changing customer demands.

3. <u>Maximizing ROI</u>: By regularly evaluating marketing efforts and making data-driven decisions, companies can optimize their marketing investments for higher returns.

4. <u>Enhancing Customer Experience</u>: Continuous improvement fosters better customer engagement by tailoring marketing messages and experiences to customer preferences.

5. <u>Identifying New Opportunities</u>: Regularly analyzing marketing data helps identify new market opportunities and potential niches for agrochemical products.

Strategies for Continuous Improvement of Agrochemical Marketing:

1. <u>Data Analysis and Insights</u>:

  - Regularly analyze marketing data, including sales figures, website analytics, social media metrics, and customer feedback.

  - Extract actionable insights to inform marketing strategies.

2. <u>A/B Testing and Experimentation</u>:

- Conduct A/B tests to compare different marketing elements, such as ad copies, visuals, and call-to-action buttons.

- Use test results to refine marketing materials and optimize performance.

3. Customer Surveys and Feedback:

- Gather customer feedback through surveys and feedback forms.

- Use customer insights to enhance product messaging and improve customer experience.

4. Competitor Analysis:

- Monitor competitor marketing strategies and initiatives.

- Identify areas where your marketing can differentiate and stand out.

5. <u>Marketing Automation and Personalization</u>:

 - Implement marketing automation tools to streamline marketing processes and improve efficiency.

 - Leverage customer data for personalized marketing campaigns.

6. <u>Content Optimization</u>:

 - Regularly review and optimize marketing content, such as website copy, blog posts, and social media updates.

 - Ensure content is relevant, valuable, and aligned with the needs of the target audience.

7. <u>Performance Tracking and Reporting</u>:

 - Establish key performance indicators (KPIs) to measure marketing effectiveness.

 - Regularly track and report on KPIs to monitor progress and identify areas for improvement.

8. <u>Agility and Flexibility</u>:

   - Stay agile and adaptable in response to changing market conditions or customer demands.

   - Quickly adjust marketing strategies as needed.

9. <u>Learning and Development</u>:

   - Invest in training and development for marketing teams to stay updated on industry trends and best practices.

   - Encourage a culture of learning and experimentation.

10. <u>Collaboration and Communication</u>:

   - Foster collaboration between marketing, sales, and product development teams.

   - Share insights and feedback across departments to inform marketing strategies.

Continuous improvement and optimization of agrochemical marketing effectiveness is a dynamic process that requires a commitment to analyzing data, embracing innovation, and adapting to the ever-changing market landscape. By continuously refining marketing strategies and customer experiences, agrochemical companies can build stronger brand connections, drive customer loyalty, and achieve sustainable growth in the competitive agricultural industry.

Chapter 12: Navigating Ethical Challenges

Error! Filename not specified.

Ethical considerations in agrochemical marketing

Ethical considerations in agrochemical marketing are essential to ensure responsible, transparent, and socially responsible practices within the agricultural industry. Agrochemical companies have a responsibility to prioritize the well-being of consumers, farmers, and the environment, and to uphold ethical standards in their marketing strategies and communications. Here's an in-depth exploration of the key ethical considerations in agrochemical marketing:

1. Safety and Health:

  - Ensuring the safety and health of farmers, consumers, and the general public is paramount in agrochemical marketing.

  - Agrochemical companies should provide clear instructions on product usage, handling, and safety precautions to minimize health risks.

2. <u>Environmental Impact</u>:

  - Agrochemical marketing must address the environmental impact of products and practices.

  - Promoting sustainable agriculture, responsible usage, and eco-friendly alternatives demonstrates ethical commitment to environmental conservation.

3. <u>Truthfulness and Accuracy</u>:

  - Ethical marketing involves providing truthful and accurate information about agrochemical products and their benefits.

  - Avoiding deceptive claims, exaggerations, and false promises ensures trust with customers.

4. <u>Transparency and Disclosure</u>:

- Transparently disclose product ingredients, potential risks, and environmental effects to enable informed decision-making by farmers and consumers.

- Clearly communicate any limitations or uncertainties associated with product effectiveness.

5. Responsible Targeting:

- Ethical agrochemical marketing avoids targeting vulnerable populations or engaging in exploitative practices.

- Adhering to responsible advertising guidelines ensures that marketing messages reach appropriate and informed audiences.

6. Supporting Sustainable Practices:

- Ethical marketing promotes and supports sustainable farming practices, such as integrated pest management and organic agriculture.

- Encouraging responsible practices enhances the overall sustainability of the agricultural industry.

7. <u>Avoiding Greenwashing</u>:

- Ethical agrochemical marketing refrains from greenwashing, which involves making misleading claims about products' environmental benefits.

- Focus on tangible and substantiated sustainability efforts.

8. <u>Respect for Local Cultures and Traditions</u>:

- Consider local cultural sensitivities and traditions when developing marketing materials and campaigns.

- Ensure that marketing strategies respect the diverse practices and beliefs of different communities.

9. <u>Data Privacy and Security</u>:

- Agrochemical companies must handle customer data responsibly and adhere to data privacy regulations.

- Obtain explicit consent for data usage and protect customer information from unauthorized access.

10. <u>Social Responsibility</u>:

   - Ethical marketing considers the broader social impact of agrochemical products on communities and society.

   - Engage in corporate social responsibility initiatives that contribute positively to the well-being of local communities and the agricultural sector.

11. <u>Ethical Advertising Practices</u>:

   - Abide by ethical advertising standards, avoiding offensive, misleading, or manipulative content in marketing materials.

   - Be respectful and honest in communications with consumers.

Ethical considerations in agrochemical marketing are not only a moral imperative but also contribute to the long-term success and sustainability of agrochemical companies. By prioritizing safety, environmental responsibility, transparency, and social impact, agrochemical businesses can build trust with their stakeholders, foster customer loyalty, and contribute to the advancement of ethical practices in the agricultural industry.

Promoting transparency and honesty

Promoting transparency and honesty in Philippine agrochemical marketing is essential to build trust among consumers, farmers, and regulatory authorities. By prioritizing transparency and honesty, agrochemical companies can establish credibility, foster positive relationships with stakeholders, and demonstrate their commitment to ethical practices. Here's an in-depth exploration of the strategies for promoting transparency and honesty in Philippine agrochemical marketing:

1. <u>Clear and Accurate Product Information</u>:
   - Provide clear and accurate information about agrochemical products, including their composition, usage instructions, safety precautions, and environmental impact.
   - Avoid making exaggerated or misleading claims about product effectiveness or benefits.

2. <u>Regulatory Compliance</u>:
   - Comply with all relevant Philippine regulations and laws governing agrochemical marketing, product labeling, and safety standards.

- Ensure that product registrations are up-to-date and aligned with regulatory requirements.

3. <u>Open Communication</u>:

 - Encourage open and two-way communication with customers, farmers, and stakeholders.

 - Address inquiries, concerns, and feedback promptly and honestly.

4. <u>Product Testing and Validation</u>:

 - Conduct rigorous product testing and validation to ensure product safety, efficacy, and compliance with quality standards.

 - Share test results and certifications with customers to enhance trust.

5. <u>Environmental Impact Reporting</u>:

- Provide transparent information about the environmental impact of agrochemical products and practices.

- Share data on product biodegradability, eco-toxicity, and contributions to sustainable agriculture.

6. <u>Responsible Marketing Messages</u>:

- Ensure that marketing messages are truthful, accurate, and supported by credible evidence.

- Avoid using language or visuals that could be interpreted as deceptive or manipulative.

7. <u>Public Disclosure of Safety Data</u>:

- Make safety data, including Safety Data Sheets (SDS), accessible to farmers, retailers, and regulatory authorities.

- Demonstrate a commitment to transparency by sharing critical safety information.

8. <u>Sustainability Efforts and Initiatives</u>:

- Highlight sustainability efforts and initiatives in marketing communications.

- Showcase responsible practices, such as integrated pest management, environmental conservation programs, and waste reduction initiatives.

9. <u>Ethical Supply Chain Practices</u>:

- Promote transparency in the supply chain, from sourcing raw materials to manufacturing and distribution.

- Ensure ethical practices and responsible sourcing of ingredients.

10. <u>Collaboration with Stakeholders</u>:

- Collaborate with farmer associations, NGOs, and government agencies to address concerns, share information, and seek feedback.

- Engaging stakeholders builds credibility and demonstrates a commitment to transparency.

11. <u>Adherence to Corporate Values</u>:

- Ensure that marketing strategies align with the company's ethical values and social responsibility commitments.

- Uphold integrity and honesty in all aspects of marketing communication.

Promoting transparency and honesty in Philippine agrochemical marketing builds a strong foundation of trust and credibility in the industry. By providing clear and accurate information, complying with regulations, and openly communicating with stakeholders, agrochemical companies can earn the respect of their customers and contribute to the sustainable growth of the agricultural sector in the Philippines. Transparency and honesty serve as guiding principles in building lasting relationships with customers and stakeholders while advancing responsible and ethical practices in agrochemical marketing.

Complying with industry regulations and standards

Complying with Philippine industry regulations and standards in agrochemical marketing is of utmost importance to ensure legal and ethical practices within the agricultural sector. The Philippine government has established strict guidelines and regulations to safeguard public health, environmental sustainability, and the welfare of farmers and consumers. Adhering to these regulations not only ensures compliance with the law but also fosters trust with customers, stakeholders, and regulatory authorities. Here's an in-depth exploration of the significance and strategies for complying with Philippine industry regulations and standards in agrochemical marketing:

Significance of Compliance with Philippine Industry Regulations:

1. <u>Legal Compliance:</u> Complying with industry regulations ensures that agrochemical companies operate within the boundaries of the law and avoid potential legal issues or penalties.

2. <u>Public Health and Safety</u>: Adhering to safety standards protects farmers, consumers, and the general public from health hazards associated with improper agrochemical usage.

3. <u>Environmental Protection:</u> Complying with regulations safeguards the environment by minimizing the negative

impact of agrochemicals on ecosystems, water resources, and biodiversity.

4. Consumer Confidence: Compliance with industry standards enhances consumer confidence in agrochemical products and strengthens brand reputation.

5. Ethical Responsibility: Complying with regulations reflects a commitment to ethical business practices, responsible marketing, and sustainable agriculture.

Strategies for Complying with Philippine Industry Regulations*

1. Stay Informed: Regularly monitor updates and changes in Philippine agrochemical regulations issued by government agencies such as the Fertilizer and Pesticide Authority (FPA)

under the Department of Agriculture (DA) and the Department of Environment and Natural Resources (DENR).

2. <u>Product Registration</u>: Ensure that agrochemical products are registered with the appropriate regulatory authorities before marketing and selling in the Philippines. Adhere to the registration requirements and submission procedures.

3. <u>Labeling and Packaging</u>: Comply with labeling requirements, including providing clear and accurate information on product labels regarding usage instructions, safety precautions, and environmental impact.

4. <u>Safety Data Sheets (SDS)</u>: Provide Safety Data Sheets (SDS) to customers, distributors, and retailers, containing essential safety and handling information for the products.

5. <u>Advertising and Promotion</u>: Adhere to advertising standards and avoid making false or exaggerated claims about product efficacy or benefits. Ensure that marketing materials align with regulatory guidelines.

6. <u>Training and Education</u>: Conduct training programs for farmers and users to educate them on proper agrochemical usage, safety protocols, and environmental protection measures.

7. <u>Environmental Impact Assessments</u>: Conduct environmental impact assessments to evaluate the potential effects of agrochemicals on the environment and take appropriate measures to mitigate risks.

8. <u>Product Testing and Quality Control</u>: Implement rigorous product testing and quality control processes to ensure that agrochemical products meet the required standards.

9. <u>Waste Management and Disposal</u>: Implement proper waste management and disposal procedures for agrochemical products, packaging, and unused materials to prevent environmental contamination.

10. <u>Regular Audits and Reviews</u>: Conduct internal audits and reviews to assess compliance with industry regulations and identify areas for improvement.

11. <u>Engage with Regulatory Authorities</u>: Collaborate with regulatory authorities to seek clarifications, guidance, and compliance assistance.

12. <u>Maintain Records:</u> Keep comprehensive records of all marketing and product-related activities, as well as interactions with regulatory bodies.

By complying with Philippine industry regulations and standards in agrochemical marketing, companies can demonstrate their commitment to responsible practices, environmental sustainability, and the well-being of farmers and consumers. Proactive compliance not only ensures legal adherence but also contributes to the development of a thriving and ethically conscious agricultural industry in the Philippines.

CONCLUSIONS

Error! Filename not specified.

1. <u>Product Positioning and Differentiation</u>: Clearly define your agrochemical products' unique value propositions and positioning in the market to stand out from competitors.

2. <u>Targeted Marketing</u>: Identify and segment your target audience, such as farmers, crop types, and regions, to tailor marketing messages and promotions effectively.

3. <u>Educational Content</u>: Provide valuable educational content, such as blogs, videos, and guides, to educate farmers about the benefits and proper usage of your agrochemical products.

4. <u>Digital and Traditional Marketing Integration</u>: Integrate digital channels like social media, email marketing, and websites with traditional marketing methods to reach a wider audience.

5. <u>Social Media Engagement:</u> Leverage social media platforms to engage with farmers, share agricultural insights, and showcase success stories using your products.

6. <u>Email Marketing and Automation</u>: Utilize email marketing and automation to keep farmers informed about product updates, promotions, and educational resources.

7. <u>SEO and Content Marketing</u>: Optimize your online presence through SEO and content marketing to increase visibility and attract a broader audience.

8. <u>Selecting the Right Distribution Partners</u>: Partner with reliable and reputable distribution partners to ensure effective product availability and reach.

9. <u>Training and Supporting Retailers</u>: Train and support retailers to enhance their product knowledge and provide better customer service to farmers.

10. <u>Channel Management Strategies</u>: Implement effective channel management strategies to optimize distribution and monitor sales performance.

11. <u>Promotional Campaigns</u>: Design impactful promotional campaigns that resonate with the Filipino agricultural community, highlighting local relevance and sustainability.

12. <u>Sponsorships and Events</u>: Participate in agricultural events, sponsorships, and trade shows to increase brand exposure and build industry relationships.

13. <u>CRM Systems for Customer Retention</u>: Utilize CRM systems to improve customer retention, track interactions, and offer personalized support.

14. <u>Personalization and Customer Support</u>: Personalize marketing messages and provide exceptional customer support to foster brand loyalty.

15. <u>Gathering Feedback and Addressing Concerns</u>: Actively gather feedback from users and address their concerns promptly to enhance product improvements and customer satisfaction.

16. <u>Embrace Sustainability Practices</u>: Promote eco-friendly features and sustainable farming practices to align with evolving customer preferences and environmental consciousness.

17. <u>Transparency and Ethical Marketing</u>: Promote transparency, honesty, and ethical marketing practices to build trust with farmers and stakeholders.

By employing these key marketing strategies, agrochemical companies can effectively promote their products, reach their target audience, and contribute to the growth and sustainability of the agricultural industry in the Philippines.

Future trends and opportunities in Philippine agrochemical marketing are likely to be influenced by advancements in technology, changing consumer preferences, and a growing focus on sustainable agriculture. As the agricultural industry evolves, agrochemical companies can seize these emerging trends to drive innovation, enhance customer engagement, and contribute to the development of a more sustainable and efficient agricultural sector in the Philippines. Here's an in-depth exploration of the future trends and opportunities in Philippine agrochemical marketing:

1. <u>Digital Transformation:</u>

- Embrace digital technologies and e-commerce platforms to streamline distribution channels and reach farmers in remote areas more effectively.

- Leverage data analytics, AI, and machine learning to gain valuable insights into customer behavior and preferences for targeted marketing.

2. Precision Agriculture and IoT:

- Integrate Internet of Things (IoT) devices and sensor technologies to enable precision agriculture practices.

- Offer smart agrochemical solutions that optimize application based on real-time data, leading to increased efficiency and reduced environmental impact.

3. Sustainable and Eco-Friendly Products:

- Develop and market agrochemical products that are environmentally friendly, biodegradable, and have minimal impact on ecosystems.

   - Highlight the sustainability features of products to align with the increasing demand for eco-conscious agricultural practices.

4. <u>Organic and Bio-Based Solutions</u>:

   - Capitalize on the growing interest in organic and bio-based agrochemical products by offering certified and effective alternatives.

   - Educate farmers about the benefits of using these solutions for sustainable crop production.

5. <u>Personalization and Customization</u>:

- Employ data-driven marketing strategies to personalize product recommendations and offers based on farmers' specific needs and preferences.

- Offer customized agrochemical solutions tailored to different crop types and local conditions.

6. <u>Direct-to-Consumer Marketing</u>:

- Explore direct-to-consumer marketing channels, such as online platforms and subscription services, to establish a direct relationship with farmers.

- Provide educational content and personalized support through these channels.

7. <u>Mobile Marketing and Apps</u>:

- Utilize mobile marketing and apps to engage farmers with real-time updates, agronomic advice, and product information on their smartphones.

- Develop user-friendly apps that facilitate easy ordering and tracking of agrochemical products.

8. <u>Integrated Pest Management (IPM) Promotion</u>:

   - Advocate for Integrated Pest Management practices that combine agrochemicals with biological and cultural controls.

   - Position agrochemical products as one component of an IPM approach to sustainable pest and disease management.

9. <u>Diversified Marketing Channels</u>:

   - Explore partnerships with e-commerce platforms, agricultural cooperatives, and retail chains to diversify marketing channels and expand product reach.

   - Collaborate with local influencers and agricultural experts to amplify marketing messages.

10. <u>Blockchain for Traceability</u>:

- Implement blockchain technology to enhance traceability and transparency throughout the agrochemical supply chain.

- Demonstrate the authenticity and origin of products to build trust with farmers.

11. <u>Climate-Resilient Solutions</u>:

- Develop agrochemical products that help farmers mitigate the impacts of climate change, such as drought-tolerant and stress-resistant crops.

- Position these products as solutions to address the challenges of changing climate conditions.

12. <u>Social and Environmental Initiatives</u>:

- Engage in corporate social responsibility initiatives that support local communities, promote sustainable farming practices, and protect the environment.

- Highlight these initiatives in marketing campaigns to resonate with socially conscious consumers.

By embracing these future trends and opportunities, agrochemical companies in the Philippines can innovate and adapt their marketing strategies to align with evolving industry dynamics and customer expectations. Building on sustainable and technology-driven practices will not only drive business growth but also contribute to the advancement of the Philippine agricultural sector while safeguarding the environment and farmer well-being.

Empowering the Philippine agrochemical industry for sustainable growth requires a collective effort from all stakeholders, including agrochemical companies, farmers, government agencies, and consumers. Sustainable growth in the agrochemical sector involves fostering environmentally friendly practices, promoting social responsibility, and ensuring economic viability for all involved. Here's an in-depth exploration of strategies to empower the Philippine agrochemical industry for sustainable growth:

1. Sustainable Product Development:

  - Invest in research and development to create innovative, sustainable, and eco-friendly agrochemical products.

  - Focus on products that minimize environmental impact, enhance soil health, and promote biodiversity.

2. Responsible Marketing and Education:

  - Practice responsible and transparent marketing by providing accurate information about products' benefits and environmental impact.

- Educate farmers about sustainable agricultural practices, integrated pest management, and proper agrochemical use.

3. <u>Collaborative Partnerships</u>:

- Foster partnerships with farmers, agricultural cooperatives, and industry associations to collectively address sustainability challenges.

- Collaborate with NGOs, research institutions, and government agencies to promote sustainable farming practices.

4. <u>Support for Smallholder Farmers</u>:

- Provide targeted support and training programs for smallholder farmers to adopt sustainable agricultural practices.

- Offer access to affordable and effective agrochemical solutions suitable for small-scale farming.

5. Data-Driven Decision Making:

   - Utilize data analytics to gain insights into customer preferences, market trends, and environmental impacts.

   - Make data-driven decisions to optimize product offerings, marketing strategies, and distribution channels.

6. Investment in Technology:

   - Embrace technology such as precision agriculture, IoT devices, and digital platforms to increase agricultural efficiency and sustainability.

   - Offer digital tools and applications that help farmers make informed decisions and improve resource management.

7. Emphasis on Soil Health:

   - Promote agrochemical products and practices that support soil health, such as organic fertilizers and soil conditioners.

- Encourage sustainable land management and soil conservation measures.

8. <u>Environmental Impact Assessment</u>:

   - Conduct rigorous environmental impact assessments for agrochemical products to identify and mitigate potential risks to ecosystems and water resources.

9. <u>Corporate Social Responsibility</u> (CSR):

   - Engage in CSR initiatives that support local communities, improve farmer livelihoods, and invest in environmental conservation efforts.

   - Communicate CSR activities to build trust and brand reputation.

10. <u>Regulatory Compliance</u>:

- Ensure strict adherence to Philippine industry regulations and standards concerning agrochemical use and marketing.

- Proactively comply with environmental and safety regulations.

11. <u>Adoption of Best Practices:</u>

- Promote the adoption of best practices in agrochemical manufacturing, packaging, and waste management to minimize environmental impacts.

12. <u>Focus on Climate Resilience:</u>

- Develop and promote agrochemical products that help farmers adapt to climate change and build resilience in their farming systems.

13. <u>Consumer Awareness and Demand:</u>

- Educate consumers about the benefits of sustainable agriculture and the role of agrochemical products in supporting eco-friendly farming.

 - Encourage consumer demand for sustainably produced food products.

14. <u>Circular Economy Initiatives</u>:

 - Implement circular economy initiatives, such as product recycling and packaging reduction, to reduce waste and resource consumption.

By implementing these strategies, the Philippine agrochemical industry can empower itself for sustainable growth that balances economic prosperity, environmental conservation, and social well-being. A commitment to sustainability and responsible practices will not only drive business success but also contribute to the long-term health and resilience of the

agricultural sector in the Philippines.